The Common Sense Early-Childhood Classroom

A Practical Guide to Caring for Preschool Children

by Barbara McCutcheon Crawford

Cover Design: Riley Wilkinson

Cover Illustration: Photos by Digital Stock

Book Design: Teena Reemer Design

© Fearon Teacher Aids
A division of Frank Schaffer Publications, Inc.
23740 Hawthorne Boulevard
Torrance, CA 90505-5927

Fearon Teacher Aids product were formerly manufactured and distributed by American Teaching Aids, Inc., a subsidiary of Silver Burdett Ginn, and are now manufactured and distributed by Frank Schaffer Publications, Inc. FEARON, FEARON TEACHER AIDS, and the FEARON balloon logo are marks used under license from Simon & Schuster, Inc.

FE11046

-To Mom and Dad—
who, by their shining example,
taught me most of what I know
about dealing with children.

-And to Jeff and Matt—
who have spent their whole lives
teaching me about children
and helping me
pass on the legacy.

3

Acknowledgments

Who we are and what we think are in part determined by the people with whom we interact. I have had the privilege over the years of working with many wonderful teachers. I express my appreciation to all of them for what they have taught me, but especially to my current staff for their support while writing this book. Thank you Linda Berrevoets, Cecilia Covino, Pat Geisel, Barbara Mentesana, and Mary Monahan.

Thank you, too, to all of the children who over the years have attended Jugtown Mountain Nursery School; I have learned something from each and every one of you. For reading drafts of my manuscript, thank you to Andrea Toth and Mary Monahan.

To Robert Elman, whose inspiration and guidance was invaluable, a mere thank you is overshadowed by the countless important hours spent reading, editing, discussing ideas, mentoring, and encouraging a fledgling writer. A special thanks to my editor, Ginger Murphy, for believing in me. Thank you to Richard, my always supportive husband and steadfast partner, for his loving patience and encouragement.

4

Contents

Introduction

There are many excellent resource books to show us how to teach colors, shapes, numbers, letters and other academic concepts to young children, but it takes special care and knowledge to teach children what is especially important: how to live a balanced, meaningful, successful, constructive, happy life. This goal, although consistent with the beliefs of many who work with children, is not discussed in my opinion as often as it should be in educational circles with reference to young children.

If I could only teach one thing to a child, I would choose the keys to a successful life. Ralph Waldo Emerson echoed this thought when he wrote:

To laugh often and much;

To win the respect of intelligent people

and the affection of children;

To earn the appreciation of honest critics

and endure the betrayal of false friends;

To appreciate beauty, to find the best in others;

To leave the world a bit better,

whether by a healthy child, a garden patch,

or a redeemed social condition;

To know even one life has breathed easier

because you have lived.

This is to have succeeded.

These are wonderful ideals, but how do they relate to the teaching of young children? Much of what I learned in school years ago is now outdated—some of what I learned is downright wrong. This may be true for others of you as well. For a teacher to work successfully in a preschool classroom, she must learn more than the contents of the curriculum. If new generations of children are to succeed in life, they must be taught how to learn and confidently solve problems using reason and critical thinking. The first step in this important journey is to become the best person a child knows how to be.

The essence of this sentiment is described well by Robert Fulghum in *All I Really Need to Know I Learned in Kindergarten* (which is reprinted here with permission):

I realized then that I already know most of what's necessary to live a meaningful life—that it isn't all that complicated. I know it. And have known it for a long, long time. Living it—well, that's another matter, yes? Here's my Credo:

ALL I REALLY NEED TO KNOW about how to live and what to do and how to be I learned in kindergarten. Wisdom was not at the top of the graduate-school mountain, but there in the sandpile at Sunday School. These are the things I learned:

Share everything.
Play fair.
Don't hit people.
Put things back where you found them.
Clean up your own mess.
Don't take things that aren't yours.
Say you're sorry when you hurt somebody.
Wash your hands before you eat.
Flush.
Warm cookies and cold milk are good for you.
Live a balanced life—learn some and think some and draw and paint and sing and dance and play and work every day some.
Take a nap every afternoon.
When you go out into the world, watch out for traffic, hold hands, and stick together.
Be aware of wonder. Remember the little seed in the Styrofoam cup: The roots go down and the plant goes up and nobody really knows how or why, but we are all like that.
Goldfish and hamsters and white mice and even the little seed in the Styrofoam cup—they all die. So do we.
And then remember the Dick-and-Jane books and the first word you learned—the biggest word of all—LOOK.

Everything you need to know is in there somewhere.
The Golden Rule and love and basic sanitation.
Ecology and politics and equality and sane living.

8

Take any one of those items and extrapolate it into sophisticated adult terms and apply it to your family life or your work or your government or your world and it holds true and clear and firm. Think what a better world it would be if we all—the whole world—had cookies and milk about three o'clock every afternoon and then lay down with our blankies for a nap. Or if all governments had as a basic policy to always put things back where they found them and to clean up their own mess.

And it is still true, no matter how old you are—when you go out into the world, it is best to hold hands and stick together.

These ideas ring true with anyone who has ever worked with young children in a classroom; for that matter, for anyone who has ever been a child. This book was written by one teacher who, over twenty-five years of working with children, has distilled her thoughts into a practical philosophy through trial and error in the classroom. This philosophy is still evolving and may someday reach wisdom, but the process itself is an exciting, illuminating experience. I have never had a boring day working with children.

Over the years that I have had the privilege of working in an early childhood classroom, one fact has become very apparent: children grow and develop with or without our input. However, without the help and guidance of the adults who care about them, children cannot fulfill their potential. With the help of teachers and parents working together, they can flourish. It is with this partnership in mind that this book was written.

As adults who work with children, teachers and parents are constantly making decisions about what to teach, how to answer the questions of a child in the best way, or how to handle a disturbing behavior. Often we find ourselves lacking the necessary information or skills to solve our problems. *The Common Sense Early-Childhood Classroom* was written to help you develop a philosophical framework useful in making these thought-provoking and worrisome day-to-day decisions.

This book is intended to provide information directly to parents and teachers, but may also serve as a resource for teachers trying to communicate with parents (and vice versa) about what happens in an early childhood classroom and why it should be that way. Communicating in a positive and productive way with parents helps foster a parent/teacher partnership that is vitally necessary for the optimal development of each child in your care.

9

Part One of the book is an explanation of my philosophy and the teaching methods it endorses. Chapter 1 presents the assumptions about children and teaching that are basic to the information in this book, along with the resulting goals and objectives. Chapter 2 contains descriptions of the developmental characteristics of two to six-year-olds. Knowing whom you are dealing with is crucial to doing an excellent job of teaching. Chapter 3 deals with the practical aspects of teaching. Chapter 4 delineates how to build an atmosphere of caring and sharing in your classroom.

Part Two explores the development of selfhood through ways to encourage a healthy self-image, the importance of developing independence in all areas in the life of a child, social/emotional conflicts and problems that may be faced by a child, and other developmental issues.

Part Three includes chapters on the ever-popular topic of changing children's behavior. It discusses basic techniques for changing behavior, explores the problems of power struggles between children and adults, examines aggressive behavior, and discusses various other negative behaviors that crop up when adults interact with children.

Part Four is all about communication: the basic techniques of effective communication, talking with children so they will listen, and communicating with parents and other professionals.

Last but not least is Part Five, which is a list of resources for those of you who would like to explore a topic in more detail. Included are books, journals, and organizations which can provide an ongoing source of current information.

- Barbara McCutcheon Crawford

10

PART ONE

Philosophy
and
Teaching Methods

Chapter 1

Assumptions, Goals, and Objectives

Most of us act on what we believe in, either consciously or unconsciously. Those of us who work with children act on our beliefs about what children are like, how children learn, and assumptions about what are the best ways to teach. It is always beneficial for teachers and parents to clarify their beliefs about children.

In this section I will share with you my beliefs with the intention of helping you to clarify your own personal beliefs about children. I believe it is crucial that those of us interacting with children be constantly mindful of how our actions impact the children that we work with. It is not realistic to assume that at every moment a teacher would stop and think out in detail all of the ramifications of what she is about to say or do. As human beings we often simply react out of habit to everyday common occurrences. It is at that time especially when it becomes even more important that we have a clear idea of our goals.

While on the job in the classroom, a teacher maintains a certain state of mind—an intuitive place where he can comfortably function within the parameters of his beliefs through conversation and actions shared with students, co-workers, parents, and the outside community. The teacher we label as an excellent teacher is one who can successfully communicate this philosophy to everyone around him.

As you read through my assumptions about children and teaching, stop and reflect upon what you have read. These ideas have been refined over many years of classroom experience. You may agree or disagree with what is written, but most importantly, you must use only that which you personally believe in, if you wish to teach with honesty and integrity.

Assumptions About Children

Children are basically good and can be trusted. Misbehavior is often caused by children acting out emotional upsets with which they are struggling; or they are signaling to the teacher that too many or unreasonable demands are being made by the teacher.

Children are intrinsically motivated to learn and will select the proper task to accomplish a particular learning if it is available to them. Part of a teacher's job is to observe the child closely enough so that items or support are provided whenever needed. Very young children have difficulty verbalizing their needs and understanding non-verbal messages. It is therefore crucial that teachers prepare the environment well and observe constantly to make adjustments that allow for maximum learning.

Each child is a unique integrated individual, learning at different rates, using her own learning style. A child will achieve in proportion to his ability, differing from other children of the same age—and even from himself at different times in his life.

Children learn by doing—play is the work of the child. Their world is firmly grounded in the concrete, and consequently, so is their thinking. Manipulations of objects of all kinds and in all combinations is extremely important in building a conceptual framework necessary for the extension and elaboration of their logical mental structures. The more senses involved, the better; for learning conducted in several modalities is sure to be more meaningful, more useful, and more long-lasting.

Making a self-portrait is a favorite activity and lets the children express their own style.

Goals and Objectives

GENERAL:

❤ To support the development of the whole child physically, emotionally, and intellectually

❤ To help the child structure her universe (or live within her environment) so that she will be successful in interacting with others, objects, and ideas; thereby forming a strong positive self-concept

❤ To encourage interactions leading each child to a clearness and understanding concerning himself which will lend itself to an inner peace and happiness

❤ To provide each child with the best opportunities for acquiring the knowledge and understanding necessary to participate competently, according to his or her ability, in the social, cultural, and economic requirements of a changing world

❤ To develop a classroom atmosphere of:
  ◆ firmness and consistency containing limits when necessary
  ◆ warmth

13

- ◆ respect for others and property
- ◆ understanding and patience
- ◆ accepting a child as she is, including strong feelings (both positive and negative), giving her a sense of well-being and a feeling of belonging
- ◆ encouraging independence and self-discipline

SPECIFIC:

"Feeling Happy"
Kara
Age 4-1/2

♥ To produce children who:

- ◆ feel happy, successful, and confident
- ◆ have wholesome attitudes toward life and learning
- ◆ are self-disciplined
- ◆ are independent thinkers
- ◆ are self-motivated and continuous learners
- ◆ can solve problems and answer questions in their own lives
- ◆ have the ability to observe, think, and judge
- ◆ can complete a task successfully
- ◆ can learn to live with and accept responsibility for their choices
- ◆ can maintain a balance of individualism and group membership
- ◆ recognize the needs and abilities of others
- ◆ can cooperate and maintain friendships
- ◆ speak or write because they need to record and communicate their thoughts
- ◆ can listen to other points of view with an open mind before making decisions or judgments
- ◆ understand and use their bodies effectively and creatively
- ◆ have an appreciation for the creative arts
- ◆ are competent in the fundamental academic skills

14

Assumptions About Teaching

Teaching is a fluid activity that goes on all through the day. We don't just teach lessons; we are teachers at all times when in the presence of children. School is an integral part of a child's life and should be an enjoyable, enriching experience, not an academic intrusion.

The environment is crucial in encouraging and fostering learning. A child must have available all the necessary resources in order to pursue his or her learning in any specific area. The teacher is a resource person and a facilitator of learning who creates an environment where learning can freely take place. She structures the classroom activities to encourage children to feel comfortable enough to pursue problems and answer their own questions. Although many decisions are made democratically by the class, the teacher as the adult remains in authority, sharing the wisdom and knowledge of a lifetime of experience. Children learn by example, the teacher being the prime adult example throughout the school day. Therefore teachers must do their best to live by the rules and ideals that are being taught to the children.

Children should be given as much freedom and responsibility as they can handle. Very young children need firm but reasonable limits and guidelines to practice and learn appropriate behaviors in many situations. As they become more capable and responsible, more freedom can be given. Some children become independent very early in life, while others gain those capabilities much later. Some require adults to provide more structure for them until they are ready to develop structure on their own. A teacher or parent must be very careful to encourage independence with as little risk of failure as possible.

Success is an integral part of learning and life. Never push a child to risk failure unless there is a reasonable chance of success. This will build the child's positive feeling about herself. The self-confident, self-accepting child has the strength to fail and not be harmed by it.

Because learning is child-centered and flows from the child, a rigidly set curriculum is not appropriate or desirable. A theme-based plan is very helpful for organizational purposes. It is invaluable for the teacher to have a vast amount of curriculum resource materials on file and ready for use at a moment's notice. It is also necessary to have developmental skill or competency hierarchies available so that a teacher can help a student progress appropriately.

Each child should be evaluated against himself or herself on his or her mastery of subject matter or on other competencies. In the early childhood years I do not believe grades which compare one child to another serve any purpose but to encourage and maintain unnecessary competitive feelings. Motivation should be toward attainment of knowledge and excellence, not becoming better than one's classmates.

Periodic constructive evaluation should be carried out by the teacher and the child, and be reported to parents by both. In order to make such a system work, careful record-keeping must be done. I would include the following in each child's portfolio: a developmental checklist, checklists of specific competencies attained within each subject area (for older children), samples of written and creative work chosen by the teacher and/or the student, and subjective evaluations done by the teacher and student if appropriate. This file would, of course, be open to teachers, parents, and the child. In such an atmosphere, evaluation becomes something constructive to be sought by the child as an aid to further progress in his or her work rather than a judgment to be feared.

Parent conferences are an important means of communication and should include the child whenever it would be meaningful and constructive.

16

Chapter 2

Developmental Characteristics of Preschoolers

In order to teach children well it's important to understand who they are, where they are coming from, and where they are going developmentally. Study of the current knowledge of child development will prove invaluable in dealing more effectively with young children.

For a good many years, I have taught three and four-year-olds on alternate days in the same classroom. Over the years I have been asked how I keep my classes straight. Even if I walked into the classroom with the wrong lesson plans in my head, it would become glaringly obvious in a very short period of time that I was in the wrong class for those plans. Any teacher who has tried it will tell you that appropriate activities for threes and fours are not very interchangeable. Three-year-olds and four-year-olds are categorically different. Each period of development has its own tasks to accomplish.

Human development research tells us that children pass through predictable stages in a continuous process during the first nine years of life. All children develop in their own individual way centered around trends in development that follow a universal sequence—with similar behaviors occurring at various levels or stages. There is a natural alternation between periods of equilibrium and disequilibrium while new behaviors are forming. Knowing why the resistance or difficulty occurs and that it is just a temporary stage helps teachers and parents cope with the ups and downs of dealing with young children.

Generalized descriptions and lists of behaviors and skills to expect at certain ages can be helpful tools if it is remembered that it is more important to understand the patterns and nuances of growth than whether a behavior is occurring exactly on time in the schedule of development. Each child unfolds in his or her own time. As long as it is a positive growth direction and falls within the wide range of normal parameters, there is nothing to be worried about.

In the following pages I have attempted to describe characteristic behaviors of two to six-year-olds. The experience of teachers like myself and the research of early childhood experts have shown the universality of developmental stages. Lists of development for each age group can be found in many books available on child development (particularly those listed at the end of this chapter). But, and this is a very big but, remember that the children do not read these books. They simply develop in their own way at their own pace in their own time.

As parents and teachers, we need to have the patience and wisdom to observe and study children so that we will better understand where they are coming from and where they are going. Then, and only then, will we be able to best teach them in a developmentally appropriate way. If you use the information provided in the developmental lists as a guide rather than as standards by which to measure children, you will be more successful in your interactions.

Two-Year-Olds

Two-year-olds have reached a level of maturity that allows them to be more sure of themselves than earlier in their lives. Emotionally, they are better able to wait and make it through small frustrations.

They learn through exploration using their curiosity and imaginations. Around two, children begin to divide objects into categories. They are becoming more familiar with symbols and language.

At about two-and-a-half years of age a period of disequilibrium occurs—affectionately nicknamed by some as "the Terrible Twos." During this time a child first truly understands that he is separate from his parents. Children of this age assert their newfound autonomy by frequently using the word, "No!" They want exactly what they want exactly when they want it and they love to resist. They are rigid and demanding, often with extremes of emotion. Complicating the situation and possibly causing some of the upheaval, they have a hard time choosing between opposite positions, such as "I want—I don't want."

The following abilities are commonly exhibited by the time a two-year-old turns three:

Gross Motor: Catches a rolled ball and returns it; throws objects a short distance; jumps with two feet; begins to hop; walks on tip toe; claps to music; walks up and down stairs with both feet on each step; puts on simple garments, such as a cap or slippers.

Fine Motor: Paints with large brush; tears paper; turns pages one at a time; colors with large crayons or markers; strings several large beads; builds a six-block tower.

Language: Uses short sentences to communicate needs and answers questions; repeats parts of songs and fingerplays; listens to short stories; follows simple directions; names self and common objects.

18

Cognitive: Imitates adults and other children; exhibits simple symbolic play (pretends a block is a car); draws a face; follows simple game rules; can group things by size; understands waiting for a turn; has the concepts of one and two.

Three-Year-Olds

Three-year-olds are no longer toddlers, but they are not yet four-year-old preschoolers; yet at any given time their behavior will range between the two extremes. Our expectations should allow for two-and-a-half-year-old behavior at times, followed shortly thereafter by more sophisticated four-year-old behavior.

Three-year-olds love to conform, cooperate, and please. They like to have friends and generally be with others. This gives them plenty of opportunity to use their newly developed language skills. Calm is a good word to describe the three-year-old. It's almost as though they are sitting back and absorbing what is going on in the world around them.

At three-and-a-half, when a new state of disequilibrium begins, a child will resist again and become strong-willed. Emotionally, three-year-olds are very unsure of themselves, wondering if they are lovable. They don't like being ignored, but when made the center of attention, they don't like others looking at them or laughing at them either.

The following abilities are commonly exhibited by the time a three-year-old turns four:

Gross Motor: Catches a large ball from six feet away; throws objects five to eight feet; improves jumping and hopping; walks on tip toe; claps to music; can walk forward and backward on a line; rides a tricycle.

Fine Motor: Makes balls and snakes with clay; pastes with one finger; strings smaller beads; uses scissors (but not on lines); laces, screws and unscrews; no longer holds a crayon with fist; copies lines and circles and crosses.

Language: Uses longer sentences and can carry on a conversation; uses pronouns appropriately; memorizes four-line songs; follows two-step directions; understands prepositions and opposites; uses adjectives and adverbs; can name many objects; recounts events of the day.

Cognitive: Asks questions; can place three pictures in sequence; can identify what's missing out of a picture; draws a face with stick arms and legs; can pair objects that are related by use; can pick out what doesn't belong in a group.

Four-Year-Olds

Four-year-olds attack the world. They have to try everything and push to the limit. They can be extremely loud or silly or boastful or angry. Even gross motor activity can be in the extreme—kicking, hitting, running, rushing, and throwing sticks and stones. A four-year-old will try to defy adult authority at times and act tough. Most often this is a way to try out different behaviors rather than a purposeful attempt to rebel. Children at this stage seem to be happy with themselves and are expanding their concepts of what they can do. Four-year-olds, although somewhat unpredictable, are a lot of fun to be with because they are always doing, questioning, and learning.

**Katie E.
Age 4**

At four-and-a-half to five, another period of disequilibrium occurs that resembles the extreme emotions of "the Terrible Twos." Four-and-a-half-year olds want to have the most, be loved the most, and generally be first in everything. Everyone else is to blame because they can't stand not being right and always need to win. If things go well they are delightful—but if not, then be ready for lots of tears and tantrum-type behavior.

The following abilities are commonly exhibited by the time a four-year-old turns five:

Gross Motor: Catches a ball away from body with hands only; throws a ball with direction; bounces and catches a ball; moves around quickly and with relative ease; rides a bicycle with training wheels; likes climbing.

20

Fine Motor: Uses scissors and can cut on the lines of simple shapes; draws with more confidence and representations; paints and colors more skillfully; buttons and zips and buckles; puts on shoes; does a puzzle of eight to ten pieces.

Language: Speaks in ten-word sentences; can listen for ten minutes and can retell a story; contributes in discussions; carries on lengthy conversations; identifies many letters of the alphabet (especially those in his/her name); can identify rhyming words; can recognize initial sounds; likes new words, especially big or silly ones; questions constantly—especially why.

Cognitive: Asks questions; can place three pictures in sequence; can identify what's missing out of a picture; draws a face with stick arms and legs; can pair objects that are related by use; can pick out what doesn't belong in a group; classifies by size, shape, color, and texture; can order and compare by size; counts from one to five; understands ordinal positions first through fifth; can solve simple verbal math problems.

Five-Year-Olds

Five-year-olds are calm, social, friendly, and very at ease with themselves. They are not demanding and love to help, please, and obey. This makes Mom (or Dad) very important now because he or she is the perfect person with whom to practice all of these new behaviors. Five-year-olds like to be taught and love getting permission to do things, making them a real pleasure to work with for teachers.

The following abilities are commonly exhibited by the time a five-year-old turns six:

Gross Motor: Reaches with dominant hand; works from left to right; uses a ball with control; can run, hop, jump, and skip; begins to distinguish left from right; understands relative positions, such as above/below.

Fine Motor: Uses scissors with control; uses a knife and fork; does a puzzle with ten or more pieces; prints first name from memory; prints numerals from 1 to 5.

Language: Can tell a story in order; recalls main ideas from a story or picture; takes turns in a group discussion; expresses emotions with words; identifies letters; matches initial letter with beginning sound; uses sound or visual clues to figure out new words; associates printed word with object; tells words that begin with the same sound; has a number of sight words; recognizes final sounds in spoken words.

Cognitive: Is able to work at a quiet, sitting activity for 15 to 20 minutes; is able to complete a task; recalls information previously taught; knows lots of personal information; can identify numerals and count ten objects; can classify by color, size, shape, pitch, and texture; can compare and estimate.

References

Ames, Louise Bates, Ph.D., Clyde Gillespie, B.S., Jacqueline Haines, A.B., and Frances L. Ilg, M.D. *The Gesell Institute's Child From One to Six: Evaluating the Behavior of the Preschool Child*. New York, NY: Harper and Row, 1979.

Bredekamp, Sue. *Developmentally Appropriate Practice in Early Childhood Programs Serving Children from Birth Through Age 8*. Washington, D.C.: National Association for the Education of Young Children, 1993.

Brazelton, T. Berry, M.D. *Touchpoints—Your Child's Emotional and Behavioral Development*. Reading, Massachusetts: Addison-Wesley, 1992.

Coletta, Anthony J. and Kathleen, *Year 'Round Activities for Two Year Old Children, Year 'Round Activities for Three Year Old Children, Year 'Round Activities for Four Year Old Children, and Year 'Round Activities for Five Year Old Children*. West Nyack, NY: The Center for Applied Research in Education, 1986.

Chapter 3
Teaching Methods and Techniques

Classroom Methods

All rules of behavior you establish in the classroom should reflect your objectives and your teaching goals. Each rule should be established for a reason that a child can fully understand. Our priority is not to have a quiet, orderly classroom because the teacher says so. We should rather strive for an atmosphere of warmth, respect, order, and joy in intellectual pursuit. If children are allowed, with guidance, to participate in the process of "creating" rules, force is never needed to enforce these rules in an early childhood classroom, for the children want them also.

♥ Ground rules should be set up right from the start, including safety precautions and the following:

◆ Unnecessary running indoors or any unsafe play is not allowed.

◆ Everyone in the classroom is to be respected, both their bodies and their feelings.

◆ All property in the classroom is to be treated with respect.

◆ Everyone must cooperate.

◆ New rules are to be made as needed (by the children and the teachers).

♥ Children should have freedom of movement except when inappropriate, such as during a presentation, a show, or a story.

♥ Open discussion should be encouraged as a regular part of each day during small group or whole class meetings.

♥ A school group is a form of family where learning is a part of living— and people, including teachers, treat one another with warmth and respect. We teach one another how to treat each other.

♥ Flexibility is a key word for teachers in this environment as the children's work is individualized by level of maturity.

♥ With the child providing the cues, the teacher should seek opportunities to promote growth in all areas. Guidance is accomplished mainly through suggestion, rather than providing

answers. A child should be allowed to discover in a situation created by the teacher for such a purpose.

❤ As many concrete and sensory experiences as possible should be provided for the children.

❤ Children should receive lots of sincere praise and verbal encouragement. These social rewards and the intrinsic rewards of learning successfully are usually enough.

❤ Socio-dramatic play is extremely important and should be encouraged and incorporated into many classroom activities.

Ground Rules for Teaching

❤ Be clear and consistent in your expectations of the children.

❤ Give plenty of feedback. With fair warning, children will have a good chance at successful behavior.

❤ Follow through on what you say and do.

❤ Be firm, warm, and logical—these qualities are not mutually exclusive.

❤ Be positive in your attitude.

❤ Be proactive by intervening when you see signs that a child is going to misbehave before she actually does. Give clues as to how to behave correctly, and then let the child do so with your praise.

❤ Be flexible within the philosophical structure of your beliefs and principles.

❤ Make time for what is important.

❤ Always remain a learner, for teaching is a creative process in which development is continual.

❤ Don't typecast children; people can change.

❤ Be open to the children and really listen.

❤ When a relationship goes wrong with a child, you own fifty percent of the problem.

❤ Emotionally, children should know what to expect from their teachers. Personal problems should be checked at the door with gum and raisins.

♥ The pendulum of popular behavior and educational theories swings both ways over time. There must be a balance in what you do. Use whatever works for you and the child. There is not just one right way to do things.

♥ Your classroom should reflect your vision of the world. Everyone involved should have a clear and reasonably accurate understanding of your attitudes and standards.

How to Structure Lessons

It is desirable to foster a peaceful, cooperative, helpful atmosphere in your classroom. How do you structure lessons so that they reflect these goals? A lesson time, by its very nature, is a structured time when a teacher can impart information to the children or encourage learning.

The movement of ideas is classically from the teacher to the child, although learning doesn't always have to be accomplished in this traditional manner. The responsibility for imparting information is still on the shoulders of the teacher, as it should be, but she doesn't always need to be the sole source of information. Information may come from many places. Books, filmstrips, videos, charts, and pictures have always made learning more interesting and less teacher-centered. Hands-on manipulation and experimentation with real objects creates greater motivation for paying attention and learning. There may be children in the class or parents who have a wealth of knowledge on a particular subject and are willing to share with the children.

The one thing that remains the job of the teacher, however, is to structure the classroom and the materials available so that the learning he wants to occur will take place. Providing many books, pictures, and objects on a topic will spur interest and discussion. The teacher becomes a resource person and a facilitator of learning. The teacher's responsibility is to provide the guidance necessary for learning to occur in a meaningful and efficient manner.

Knowledge is immediately meaningful when the children act out what they are learning.

© Fearon Teacher Aids FE11046

Chapter 4

Creating a Peaceful Classroom

Going to a day care center or nursery school is a new and unique experience for most children. For many, it is the first time away from Mom or Dad for an extended period of time. Therefore it is crucial that the time away take place in a warm, nurturing, and supportive environment. A child's first experience with school should be enjoyable and enriching.

Children Learn by Example

Children learn by doing. "Play is the work of the child," Maria Montessori wisely stated. Their world is firmly grounded in the concrete, and consequently, so is their thinking. Activities should be planned to allow the child, who is intrinsically motivated to learn, the freedom at times to select the appropriate materials to accomplish a particular learning. The classroom should be structured enough to encourage children to feel comfortable pursuing problems and answering their own questions. The teacher should create a challenging yet non-threatening environment that fosters learning and provides a reasonable chance for success.

Children should be given as much freedom and responsibility as they can handle. Very young children need firm but reasonable limits and guidelines to practice and learn appropriate behaviors.

The atmosphere that you create in a classroom is extremely important. Children learn by example. Everything you say and do will affect how children think and what they will learn. No one is perfect, nor is such perfection desirable, but it is necessary to realize the effect that teacher behavior has on children. Children model behavior they see, especially the behavior of adults they respect.

You will want to develop an atmosphere of firmness and consistency with reasonable limits. The classroom should be a place of warmth, understanding, and patience where the norm is respect for people and property. In school a child should be accepted as she is, including strong feelings, both positive and negative. This will give the child a sense of well-being and a feeling of belonging. In this way you will encourage independence and self-discipline.

Preschool children do notice differences in people—physical, cultural, and emotional. How the children handle these differences depends on what they have been taught. Children who are taught to respect and appreciate differences will generally not tease or belittle. Prejudice is taught and, in my opinion, can be undone, particularly in very young children. Teach that we are all different and have different ideas, and that these differences are okay and wonderful. This reminder works very well when one child criticizes another for making a mistake. If it is

"Hello, everybody, yes indeed...." Circle time instills a feeling of community in the classroom.

merely a different way of doing something, you can explain that "Julie's idea about how to _____ is different from yours. It's okay for people to have different ideas."

When explaining differences such as "Why does he have a penis?" or "How come Juan's legs don't work?" be matter-of-fact about body parts and anything else you might need to express. This puts the difference in perspective and stresses that it is not the most important characteristic of that person.

To a child, adults seem to be perfect and can do everything right. It is important that children realize adults can and do make mistakes, too. Whenever I make a mistake in my classroom I immediately point it out. The importance of this to the children was brought home to me one day by a five-year-old in my class. Allen, who is well known to the staff for his mistakes, was minding his own business at the snack table when I knocked an entire glass of juice all over the table. With a knowing grin on his face, he nodded yes and said to the child sitting next to him, "It's okay. Teachers make mistakes, too." And it was okay.

Teaching Through Curriculum Centers

A manageable and appropriate way of introducing young children to interesting, important concepts is through classroom curriculum centers—spaces in the classroom devoted to certain topics or themes—each full of materials appropriate to the subject.

The curriculum of a center is based upon knowledge of development in major learning areas: fine motor, gross motor, social/emotional, and cognitive (how a child thinks, how she expresses herself, and what facts she knows). A list of your learning objectives in each area will make planning more efficient.

Space often does not permit all centers to be in operation at once in your classroom, nor is this likely to be desirable. All materials should be readily available for use with little or no preparation. My favorite way to organize and store curriculum materials is in cardboard file boxes with lids, one for each theme or unit. The unit boxes can be taken out as designated by your lessons and/or interest of the children.

As far as physical setup of the classroom is concerned, it may be wise to have a few centers where complete changes of equipment and materials are an expected part of the classroom organization. This will allow you to meter the use of some of the less popular centers and to introduce as many special-interest centers as are needed. It will also maintain a sense of continuity and security, as these changes are expected by the children. The rest of the classroom centers can be permanent, although you may want to vary their contents to reflect themes or needs of students.

There is no ideal way to set up the centers or areas in a classroom, because each class is unique and composed of many different individuals. A classroom should be tailored to the class that uses it and evolve with the growth of the children—and the teachers. For example, one term your class may be doing a lot of work in the block area while the next term, or even the next week, there is only minimal interest. It is therefore to your advantage as creator and caretaker of the classroom environment to delete, minimize, enlarge, or add centers as student interests and needs may dictate.

The following are what I consider the basic classroom areas or centers and a list of recommended contents.

Building with blocks requires physical coordination, logical/mathematical thinking and the cooperation of all involved.

28

BLOCK AREA:

Develops motor coordination and creativity in building, allows some socio-dramatic play, encourages cooperative endeavors requiring verbal communications, facilitates intuitive concrete learning of mathematical relationships

- ♥ Large hollow blocks for building (can be cardboard)

- ♥ Variety of wooden blocks in all shapes and sizes(ideal is a set of unit blocks)

- ♥ Cars, trucks, planes, vehicles of all types, and traffic signs

- ♥ Stacking boxes for pretend driving and riding

- ♥ Play people and animals

- ♥ Small doll-size play buildings with furniture

There is nothing more satisfying than putting the last block on a building that doesn't fall down.

PLAYHOUSE/SOCIO-DRAMATIC PLAY AREA:

Encourages role playing of all kinds, requires cooperation for maximum enjoyment, provides a relatively safe outlet for exploring and understanding strong feelings

- ♥ Kitchen, bedroom, and (if space permits) living room furniture, plus dishes, pots, pretend food, dolls and doll clothes

- ♥ Dress-up clothes of all kinds, including tools/utensils of as many professions as possible

- ♥ Full-length mirror of polished aluminum

- ♥ Any objects that would lend themselves to creative dramatic play, such as telephones, cash registers, picnic baskets, wigs, etc.

LIBRARY AREA/BOOK CORNER:

A place to escape from the noise and tumult of the classroom, a resource center for answers to questions, a place to read or just think. You may want more than one book corner. Books may be included in many centers—reference/science books in the science center, good stories on tape in the listening center, books that go with puppets or stuffed animals in the language center, counting and number books in the math center, alphabet books In the ABC center

- ♥ A rug and comfortable cushions or chairs and a table

- ♥ Books, books, books, and magazines

29

❤ A fish tank, plants, pictures, posters, etc., to give a peaceful, homey feeling

ART/CREATIVE AREA:
To provide the media for self-expression

Committing ideas to paper with the stroke of a brush provides quiet joy.

❤ Paints, brushes, and easels

❤ Paper of many types

❤ Glue, paste, tape, scissors, and stapler

❤ Crayons, chalk, pencils, pens, and markers

❤ Fingerpaint, paint boxes or cakes, and tempera

❤ Clay, plasticine, and play dough

❤ String, yarn, scrap cloth, wire, styrofoam, feathers, doilies, etc., for collage

❤ A scrap box where colored paper scraps of each color can be kept in file folders or ziplock plastic bags for use in other projects

MUSIC AREA:
For creative expression through music and movement, for enjoyment and appreciation of varied types of music

❤ Rhythm and other instruments

❤ Songbooks

❤ Record (or tape) player and a collection of records (or tapes), both music and activity

❤ Tape recorder and blank tapes to record musical compositions or special performances

MANIPULATIVE AREA:
To provide lots of practice of fine motor skills in a game-like context

❤ Puzzles

❤ Building toys of all kinds

❤ Toys that require sequencing

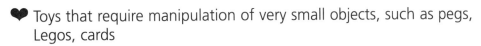

♥ Toys that require manipulation of very small objects, such as pegs, Legos, cards

♥ Lacing boards

♥ Toys that must be constructed in order to be used

LANGUAGE AREA OR WRITING/ABC AREA:

Materials to encourage verbal and written communication, to develop isolated language skills, such as listening or letter reproduction

♥ Paper, pencils, crayons, markers, scissors, tape, and stapler for creative "writing"

♥ Idea/worksheets revolving around skills being emphasized that day or week

♥ Skill games, either commercial or teacher-made

♥ Tracing and letter reproduction materials

♥ Books (or locate this area next to the Library Area)

Reading begins with "reading" the pictures in an illustrated book.

♥ Tape recorder with head sets and cassette stories/lessons (this is so popular in my classroom that it has become a separate center called the Listening Center located in what used to be a closet under the staircase)

♥ A typewriter or computer

SENSORY AREA:

To provide first-hand sensory experiences in teacher and parent-approved ways (no need to hide your water play from the teacher in the bathroom). Each of the following is to be presented one at a time on different days:

♥ A water table, tub, or large sink suitable for water play and appropriate toys to use in it

♥ Playdough, clay, or other malleable materials

♥ Fingerpaints, soap flakes, shaving cream

♥ Sand, dirt, rice, dried beans (we have an indoor sand table which is always popular)

31

MATHEMATICS AREA:

To provide lots of concrete experiences in working with number and mathematical relationships, aid in numeral identification and computation

- Numeral and number matching games

- Building blocks of all types that require the use of intuitive mathematical relationships, such as parquetry blocks

- Cuisenaire rods

- Unifix cubes

- Attribute blocks

- Dominoes

- Geometric shape discrimination games

- Materials to sort, classify, count, sequence, or pour, such as buttons, pennies, bottle caps, shaped erasers, etc.

- Rulers, numberlines, scales, balances, and other devices used to explore measurement

SCIENCE AREA:

To provide materials and tools for the exploration of the child's world, especially the natural environment (should be in close proximity to the Math Area, if not the same center)

- Animals of different species, as many as you and the children can reasonably take care of

- Appropriate pictures, charts, and books

- Anything from their environment that the children are interested in observing, manipulating, and studying

- Natural objects collected by the class

- Seeds, plants, and planting materials

- Magnifying glasses, prisms, magnets, wire and batteries

- Gears, screws, bolts, broken clocks, etc. (Be sure to keep small objects out of the reach of children younger than 3 years.)

- Valuable "junk"—the children will know what to do with it!

OUTDOOR/LARGE MOTOR AREA:

To develop balance and coordination (usually out of doors)

- ❤ Climbing structures requiring different skills

- ❤ Riding toys, such as wagons, bikes, scooters, etc.

- ❤ Balls, bats, racquets, scoops, hoops, ropes

- ❤ Sand and dirt toys

- ❤ Building things, such as boards, ramps, ladders

SPECIAL INTEREST AREAS:

To be set out for a limited amount of time when the class (or enough members of the class) is interested

- ❤ Puppet theater and puppets

- ❤ Pretend store, restaurant, train, bus, beauty parlor, etc. (can easily be incorporated in the Playhouse Area)

- ❤ Bowling game

- ❤ Papier-mâché project

- ❤ Woodworking bench

- ❤ Cooking project

- ❤ Box and cardboard construction

- ❤ Rainy-day activities to replace going out in inclement weather— Nerf balls, inflatable punching bags, tumbling mat, etc.

- ❤ Special projects of any kind

- ❤ This list is only limited by your imagination!

All aboard! A little imagination transforms four chairs, a few hats and paper tickets into the Jugtown Express Train.

Taking Turns/Waiting

"It's not fair!" How many times have you heard this in your classroom? If yours is a normal one, many more times than you would like to! The concept of fairness changes as children pass through different developmental stages. In order to help solve conflicts and teach children to share better, it is important to understand how children think and view the world around them.

At age two, only "me" exists. There is no awareness of the feelings, thoughts, or even actions of others; so there can be no representations of fairness in the behavior of toddlers.

Fair for threes is not very different. Fair is getting what I want. If both of the children in a three-year-old confrontation get what they want, they are both happy. It does not matter whether it is fair to an adult. At three, fair equals happy.

Imagine two three-year-olds playing at a sand table with four small pots and two spoons, one red and one blue. You come upon the scene as they squabble over who is playing with what. An adult stepping in might decide that sharing of the toys is what is needed, giving each child a fair share—two pots and a spoon. The possible result: two children crying. Making your presence known and patiently watching would reveal that Kim only wanted the red spoon and didn't care that Don had all of the rest of the toys.

For a four-year-old, fair is having the same kind or amount as your friends—not the broken one, not the small one, not the large one if everyone else has a small one. It is easier for adults to determine what is fair with four-year-olds because their sense of fairness is much closer to that of an adult.

"I had it first!" is a common complaint among four-year-olds. They have already learned that possession is ninety percent of the law. Unfortunately, their idea of possession extends beyond the current use of an object. A common scenario if you work with young children: John picks up a plane from the floor and begins to busily play. Judy comes into the room and is very upset that John is playing with her toy, despite the fact that she has been at the art table for more than fifteen minutes.

Five-year-olds have a wider world view. Their sense of fairness can be summed up as: "It's not fair. You had it the last three times and I never had it!" A five-year-old's concept of fairness goes beyond the event occurring at that moment. A five-year-old will take the past and the future into account when making a decision as to whether something is or isn't fair.

Keep all of this in mind as you work with children to resolve conflicts, but remember that the most important goal here is to teach children to resolve their own conflicts, not to make something fair as you see it. In a conflict situation, placing blame is not the answer, nor is it constructive. It is important to discern all the facts about exactly what happened, but not to blame the children. This information will be needed to teach the children involved how they might have better solved their problem through talking, listening and cooperating.

Waiting patiently and taking turns makes being in a group a pleasant experience. These skills do not come naturally; they are usually learned in a random and haphazard way as children proceed through childhood. We often tell children, "Be more patient," or "Wait just a minute and you'll get your turn."

Every moment in dealing with children can become a learning situation—a teachable moment. Teachers and parents can effectively teach children how to delay gratification and wait their turn. Simply break down the behavior into basic parts that can be easily understood and readily learned. Create a positive, successful experience that children will connect with waiting. Behavior that has been positively reinforced will be more likely to be repeated. Gradually lengthen the period of time to wait for gratification.

Let's apply this to a typical classroom situation. Six children are in the art area working on collages with a teacher. The materials available are precut shapes and pictures, crayons and glitter. There are dishes of shapes, pictures, and crayons in the center of the table. Glue is placed between two children with a brush for each. The glitter is available for use by one child at a time inside a dishpan large enough to hold the children's papers. Assuming that the children have already been taught how to use glue, crayons, and glitter, this is predominantly a free art activity. The teacher can then serve as a resource person and focus on teaching the children how to function effectively in the group.

Teaching in small groups makes waiting for a turn less of a challenge and creates an expectation of success.

At the art table, give out materials enough for each pair of two children to share: for example, one glue dish with two brushes in it, one set of crayons to share, or one bowl of macaronis. This limited sharing will make it easier to handle. At first this will mean that it will take more time to finish projects and will be significantly more work for the teacher involved, but the long-term effects will more than justify the energy expended.

All of the explaining and repeating about how we share materials will reinforce the idea of sharing and taking turns, so that eventually the behavior will generalize to all work done in school. You will then be able to concentrate on the actual content of what you are teaching rather than the structure of how you accomplish it. The children will already know the routine of cooperation brought about by sharing and taking turns.

In this particular collage project the teacher will tell children that everyone must wait for their turn to use the glitter. It is then important to make sure that at first the wait is short. This will create success and therefore assure repetition of the desired behavior of waiting patiently in the future.

A crucial step is the communication of what is appropriate behavior in this circumstance. "Put glue on whatever part of your collage you want to sparkle. Then come over to the dishpan, put your paper inside, sprinkle glitter on the glue, and shake the loose glitter off. What should you do if someone else is already using the glitter?"

Children will undoubtedly know the response, "Wait your turn."

"Good thinking," you reply.

You now have two choices: 1) let the children continue to generate ideas about how to behave which you then help to distill and polish; or 2) explain options for good ways to wait to help the time pass constructively:

a) Quietly wait in line

b) Watch the person ahead of you

c) Go back to the table and glue or color a little more

d) Talk quietly to a friend or the teacher

When you "catch" a child waiting appropriately, pay a verbal compliment such as, "I like the way you waited for your turn" or "Thank you for waiting patiently," or "Kristen really knows how to take turns," or "I liked the way you talked with Johnny quietly while you waited."

As soon as the behavior is completed successfully, reward the child verbally with a smile and a nod, a pat on the back, or a touch to the hand. This use of body language may seem artificial to you at first, but it is a very powerful form of communication, especially with children who are not always paying close attention to what you say.

No matter what form of recognition or reward you choose to give to a child, make sure that it is genuine. Children can see right through insincerity, although

36

they may not give you any indication. The result will be a lack of trust in what you say and what you do, making it more difficult to effectively change this child's behavior in the future. If you cannot honestly say, "I like the way you're talking to your friends (or whatever)", don't say it. Simply describe what the child has done—"You waited for your turn" or "You're painting with lots of colors." This validation by someone significant in the child's life is enough of a reward to encourage positive behavior.

Build ways to encourage taking turns and sharing into the regular activities in your classroom. Once these behaviors have been taught, the simple carrying out of routines will reinforce these desired behaviors. In the following paragraphs are examples of easy ways to foster sharing and taking turns in your classroom during activities that are probably already in your daily schedule.

During group time, pass things around for children to see, touch, smell, or whatever is appropriate for a particular lesson. Once again, this is more practice in taking turns in a structured setting. The children have the security of knowing that the teacher will make sure everyone gets their turn.

Play lots of games where children take turns being the leader or choosing what it is that you will do or sing next. Good games (or songs) for this are: *Red Light-Green Light, Hokey Pokey, Punchinella.*

Show and tell has a long-standing tradition in early childhood classrooms, and for good reason. In addition to strengthening language skills, it is the perfect vehicle for encouraging waiting your turn. It feels very good to be the center of attention in a safe, positive activity. An added benefit is the strengthening of self-esteem that occurs when all eyes are on you and you want it that way.

Sing songs where each child's name is spoken in the song. Everyone likes to hear her name out loud. Some examples of such songs are: *Hello, Everybody, Yes Indeed; Red Rover; Who Stole the Cookies from the Cookie Jar.* Many songs can be converted to this type of song with a little imagination. For example, *Here Comes Peter Cottontail* can become *Here Comes Bobby Cottontail.* If their names are in the song, the children will pay attention better and therefore learn more.

Classroom jobs are an excellent opportunity to foster responsibility and a feeling of community, while once again reinforcing the skills of waiting and taking turns.

Cook with a small group of children at a time. Taking turns is an absolute necessity here in order for the recipe to turn out right. The best part is that you can eat the project when you are finished. Cooking teaches cooperation and patient waiting.

Feeding the classroom pet is another perfect opportunity to reinforce taking turns. Keep a list near the cage of whose turn is next or incorporate turns into a job chart. All of the children want to take good care of "Fluffy" and can understand that he can only be fed once a day. The knowledge that waiting your turn is good for the pet you love makes it easy to handle the wait.

Caring for a classroom pet develops responsibility.

Have daily discussions where it is necessary to wait your turn to speak. Depending on your classroom schedule, this may be managed best at circle, snack, or during a small group activity. At first it will be necessary to make sure that every child in the group has a turn. Later on, when the skills of waiting your turn are firmly entrenched, you may introduce the idea that every person will not get to speak each time a discussion is held. Explanations that make sense to young children are: 1) If everyone speaks, it will take very long and we will have to sit quietly for a long time; or 2) If every child has a turn to talk, we won't have as much time to play outside (or whatever activity you wish to substitute).

Share your feelings about anything or an anecdote about something that happened to you recently. The simple act of conversing with a child is a good example of sharing and taking turns. Teaching by example is one of the strongest motivators.

38

PART TWO

Developing Selfhood

Chapter 5
Developing a Healthy Self-Image

Self-Esteem

There is nothing more important than having a healthy self-image. When we feel good about ourselves we are usually happy and successful at whatever we choose to do. It is important for adults to help children develop high self-esteem— a personal judgment of their worthiness. We should strive to make children feel lovable and capable.

What happens when a child makes a mistake or fails at something? A child with low self-esteem may just give up and assume "I'm not good enough to do this." A child with high self-esteem, however, will assume that she is capable, so if she fails, something else must be going wrong. She looks for what is wrong, fixes it, and then goes on, most likely to succeed. Failure for a child with high self-esteem is often just the first step to success.

Success is the best motivation for future success. This may sound simple-minded and obvious, but is very valid and effective. When we are successful at what we do, positive feelings about ourselves seem to get better. When we feel better about ourselves, we are then more likely to take risks and continue trying something new. We cannot achieve and succeed unless we are secure enough and brave enough to take some risk.

Whether a child feels loved and valued will obviously affect his development. Little things can make a big

"Laughing"
Kelsey
Age 4-1/2

difference in how loved a child will feel. Remembering that Jason's favorite color is orange and letting him have the orange ball says to him that you respect his choices and care enough about him to remember.

More examples of how to respect children's needs and choices include: putting two good friends who don't disrupt each other's learning in the same work group; not making Kirby wear a smock (even though it's the rule) because he has "a thing" about it; allowing Jennifer to say it her way instead of using your exact words; sometimes letting the children pick out what book you will read or what game will be played; and allowing children to form their own organization of materials if it does not disrupt their learning.

All of these send a message to the children on a day-to-day basis that what they think matters to you. It affirms their positive feelings about themselves and solidifies your relationship with them.

Sex-Role Stereotyping

It is beneficial for children to have a strong sense of whether they are a boy or a girl by the age of three. It is then that they begin to work on what it means to be a boy or a girl in our society. As educators, we need to not pass on gender stereotypes that will hinder a child who is developing his or her sexual identity.

Playing with dolls is terrific practice for becoming a good parent–and it's fun, too!

We must make it clear that all children, whether they are boys or girls, can be who or what they want to be. We all make choices in our lives. The children need to learn that their choices are not limited by their gender.

This is not as simple as it sounds. Sex-role stereotypes are so ingrained in all of us that we sometimes do not realize when we are inadvertently passing them on to future generations. It is so easy when a child loses a button or rips his clothing to say, "Your Mommy will fix it when you get home." This assumes that it is always the woman of the family who does the sewing. Get in the habit of saying your Mommy or Daddy in almost all instances to avoid this trap. Granted, this is a very subtle reference, but sex roles are not formally passed on; we learn them by osmosis through hundreds of daily interactions.

41

Another inadvertent way that we pass on stereotypes is by always assigning boys to traditionally male roles when we play games—such as farmer, doctor, or construction worker. We need to constantly emphasize that girls and boys can be anything they want to be as they grow up.

An even more insidious habit is assuming that a girl would rather have a more passive role than be the leader or active participant in an activity. Active/passive decisions are more a function of personality than of gender. The solution to this problem is to try to make all of your classroom decisions carefully thinking about the effect they will have on the development of all children. Obviously an impossible task, it is an ideal toward which we should strive.

Completing Tasks

Remember your parents saying, "Always finish what you begin"? How do we teach this to the children in our care? Start by making all the tasks that are presented and/or required at school of reasonable length and difficulty so that a young child can easily complete them. Use developmental norms to choose projects and tasks that are at the level of the children in a particular class. In this way, a child will experience success, feel good about herself, and most likely be motivated to gladly repeat the behavior.

Let's use the craft project of making a paper dog as an example. A three-year-old may enjoy gluing eyes, nose, and a few spots on a precut dog shape. A four-year-old might also like to color the dog and possibly glue on lots of spots. The reason these children enjoy this task is because they are able to successfully accomplish what you are asking them to do. A five-year-old could also cut out the dog shape once it is decorated. If the criteria for completion is too difficult for children's capabilities, it will result in failure, or if the task is completed, it may be accompanied by great frustration.

Gradually build on past successes by making each subsequent task a little harder. Your class will look forward to the challenge of the next project because they know you won't give them something that is going to be too difficult.

Always verbally reward a child for a job well done. "Good job," "All right!" "I liked the way you carefully finished your project," or "Great painting, John!" is enough of a social reward. Children like to know that they've done a good job and are appreciated.

42

Shy Children

To get shy children into the habit of responding when spoken to, asking for what they want, and sharing their thoughts with others, specific intervention is necessary. At first this may feel a little artificial, but will help to promote more social behavior. One technique that works is to plan for a shy child's interactions. For example, you might ask a shy child, "What would you like to do today? Would you like to play in the playhouse with Sean or build in the block area with Kimberly?" Note that each choice given to this child includes working with another child who is already involved in the area mentioned. This insures that the other child is at least interested in what you are suggesting and decreases the probability of a rejection situation.

Don't push too hard when dealing with shy children. Give them time to absorb what you are trying to do. Gradually upgrade what you ask of them by breaking their planned interactions into small do-able steps. Each time success is felt, children will be more motivated to accept the next challenge you require of them.

43

Chapter 6
Developing Independence

The best way to develop independence in children is to encourage them to do things for themselves. The difficulty is to encourage children to do things that are likely to bring success. Asking a three-year-old to tie his shoes is not appropriate. Putting shoes on the right feet is a more appropriate challenge. It's important to use developmental guidelines when deciding what tasks are appropriate for the children in your care. Developmental guidelines are mostly common sense, but presented in a very organized, specific, and helpful framework. They have been derived from years of experience and research on the behavior of young children.

Now that I'm four, I can do it myself!

Allowing children to do things on their own isn't always as easy as it sounds. A task can be completed by an adult much more quickly and efficiently. If you are pressed for time, it can be excruciatingly frustrating to wait and watch a child's fumbling and inefficient attempts to accomplish what for you is a very simple task. Don't ask a child to do something on his or her own if you do not have the time to be patient and supportive. Either plan ahead and allow for the extra time needed by the child to finish a particular task or explain to the child that it is your turn to do the task this time. They will get to do the task the next time.

Independence in the Classroom

There are many ways to foster independence in the classroom, the most important of which is creating an atmosphere of respect and acceptance. Independence is built during everyday activities—being able to do things for oneself, serving and feeding oneself, cleaning up after oneself, and helping others.

Create an environment that encourages children to do things for themselves. Place objects necessary to do a job where the children can easily find and reach

them. Use organizational methods that children can identify and remember easily. Keep items used often in the same spot in the classroom. The children should not have to think about where the scissors, the crayons, the scrap paper, or the paints can be found each day.

It also helps to use open or clear containers so that contents inside are readily visible. Most preschool children cannot read words, so labels are not useful unless they are accompanied by pictures or photographs. In no way do I mean to imply that word labels should not appear on classroom items, for children do need exposure to words, and what a fun way to do so! An inexpensive and easy way to make picture labels is to cut pictures out of catalogs, cover them with clear contact, and attach to the appropriate containers.

Having the tools children need close at hand promotes independence and enthusiasm.

Another way to foster independence is to make it easy to put items away or back on shelves. By attaching photos (or catalog pictures) to a shelf, a child can readily return an item by simply matching an item to its picture.

Make it easy to clean up after children by keeping the dustpan and brush near the sand or art table. During art, keep a sponge or wet cloth at the table for the children to use to clean up spills—or to wipe their fingers. Have trash cans strategically placed around the classroom. If you are doing a very messy project like fingerpainting, fill a dishpan with warm, soapy water and place it on a chair near the art table with a pile of paper towels. The children will be able to clean themselves and no one will have to clean all of the fingerpaint off the sinks, walls, and floor of the bathroom.

At snack time, assign the children jobs, such as passing out the napkins or snack, pouring their own juice, wiping the table, or collecting the trash. At first it might take longer while children are learning their various assignments, but they will become more efficient and even be able to eventually read what jobs are assigned from a list posted on the wall. Many of the children in my classes learn how to read the names of all of their classmates in this way.

During cleanup time, everyone should participate. It doesn't matter if a child cleans up his own mess, as long as each child does his share. Some children like to put blocks away, matching the shapes of the blocks to the shapes on the shelves, but do not enjoy block building. Develop an attitude of "we all help each other and work together."

45

Most early childhood classrooms are set up with learning centers. If the centers are organized so that it is easy to use and replace things, the children will be more likely to use the materials in appropriate and constructive ways. For example, in the dramatic play area, the dishes, silverware, pots and pans are often hard to put away. The children need an organization that helps them focus on a way to categorize things.

At our school, we put all of the cups (it doesn't matter if they all are from the same set, as long as they are cups) into one plastic basket labeled with a picture of a cup. Accordingly, plates go in one basket, silverware in another, and so forth. Each basket is then placed on the shelf on top of the appropriate matching photo. This aids the children in organizing the cleanup. One child can be in charge of cups, one in charge of plates, and so on. The problem of knowing where to start in the seemingly impossible task of putting dishes away has been alleviated. At first the children will need suggestions from the teacher about this type of cleanup, but after a while, for the most part they will be able to clean up on their own.

A dilemma often faced in a classroom with many centers is how to keep the children from using the contents of one center when that center is "closed" or not available. This might occur at cleanup time when a center is all cleaned up and you do not want the items in the center taken out again. Another instance is when all of the centers cannot be opened at the same time because there are not enough adults to supervise them well or because the use of one center, such as the music center, might be disruptive to what is going on in the rest of the classroom.

In our classroom, we use two similar signals that the children understand without the need for a teacher to say, "We're not using that center right now." The first is a flap system, where cloth flaps or curtains have been attached to the fronts of many of the shelves in the classroom. Whenever the flap is down, this is a signal that the things on that shelf are not to be used until the flap is lifted by a teacher.

Similarly, centers that have their own lights can be closed by just turning off the light. Little desk lamps or clamp-on lights can be used for this purpose. This is so simple yet so effective in cutting down the amount of teacher intervention necessary to run a classroom and has the added benefit of teaching the children to be more self-sufficient.

I tell the teachers in my school that if they are doing a good job of fostering independence with their class they will begin to feel useless around the end of March, because the children have taken on many of the responsibilities of "running" the classroom.

Motor Skills

Practice and repetition are the key factors in increasing both fine motor and gross motor skills in young children. Children naturally practice things that they need to master. Watch children playing with puzzles or manipulative games. They do the same puzzle or game over and over with relish until they are satisfied with their performance or their knowledge of the task. Watch them out of doors climbing up and jumping off the same boulder twenty times in a row until they feel confident that they have mastered it!

Children need daily opportunities to practice both fine and gross motor skills. A daily routine which includes plenty of outdoor play will encourage the use of the large muscle groups. Most children love to run, climb, swing, and generally use their whole body in play. Fine motor skills are most easily sharpened indoors—using crayons, paints, puzzles, Legos and other building toys, lacing, stringing beads, and anything else that children can do with their hands.

"I would go camping."
Paul
Age 4

As a teacher who is a facilitator of learning, you can use this mastery behavior to work for you in your curriculum. Make available games, toys, or materials that will encourage the children to practice the skills you see as necessary for their continued development. If you have chosen well, you may not even have to tell the children what to do; they will be naturally motivated to experiment and practice with the objects you have provided.

For example, if you want to develop the muscles needed to cut with scissors, you might put out matching games using clothespins in the manipulative, math, or language areas. These are homemade games where one half of the match is on the clothespin, the other is on a card to which the clothespin must be clipped at the appropriate spot. In the dramatic play area, you can put up a clothesline with clothespins to "do the wash."

47

At the sand table, you can provide tongs of all different types and sizes with "treasures" that can be hidden and found. At one table in the art area, you can put out playdough to strengthen the muscles of the fingers. At the other table, you can put out scissors and scraps of construction paper for random cutting. It will not be necessary to ask the children to practice their cutting skills. They will already have begun and will be having fun doing it! You can even ask children to tear newspaper for a papier-mâché project that you will do on another day. (Tearing uses many of the same muscles used in operating a scissors.)

Playing with masks helps children separate fantasy from reality by allowing them to take on different roles.

The same method can be used to foster gross motor development. Just make sure that the equipment is provided in a space that will be safe for its use. Unless you have a large, open gymnasium-type room at your school, rubber balls are better used outdoors. Stuffed or sponge balls can be used indoors if the children are properly trained in their safe use.

If hopping is the skill you would like to focus on, provide lots of opportunities during the week to hop. Make hopscotch grids for the children to play either with chalk outside or with tape on the floor inside. Play games where hopping can be included—like *Simon Says, Follow the Leader, Relay Races,* or *Punchinella.* Use your imagination to change the dramatic play area into Hoppingtown where everyone hops. Practicing skills can be fun.

Toilet Training

By the age of three, most children will be toilet trained. This means that they no longer wear diapers of any kind, go to the bathroom in the toilet, can do most of the toileting by themselves, and have few accidents. This is a phenomenal accomplishment and the adults around young children must remember this, especially when a child has an accident. It's easy for a child to become so involved in what she is doing that she forgets about going to the bathroom.

48

When an accident does occur, the child should be involved in the cleanup, particularly in the changing of the clothes. This should be done in a matter-of-fact manner with no hint of punishment. If the accident occurred in a group situation, the child should be allowed some privacy with you talking to the child alone. Discussing why the accident occurred can be very helpful.

Children are often not clear about why the accident happened, perhaps because they were so engrossed in what they were doing that they missed the signals from their body about its need to go to the bathroom. An appropriate suggestion might be to go to the bathroom as soon as you notice that you have to go and come back to whatever you were doing later. This isn't as obvious as you might think to a busy three-year-old.

Be sure you do not make the child feel badly because there's been an accident. Tell the child that everyone has accidents, it's O.K., and you know that she will remember the next time. Blaming and being negative never helps. What this child needs is your gentle guidance and encouragement.

It is always a good idea to be proactive and create opportunities for success. The next time you see signs that a child possibly needs to go to the bathroom (squirming, holding oneself, or hopping around) remind the child by asking, "Do you need to use the bathroom?" Then you can compliment the child for being big and responsible and doing a good job.

49

Chapter 7
Developmental Issues

Readiness

If all teachers at all levels taught using developmentally appropriate practices, every teacher would assess where each child is in every area of development and provide appropriate learning activities. Age cut-off dates would be a simple means of deciding which children would attend which schools or classes without any implication of a rating or attainment of a particular level of achievement.

Then the only readiness we would pay attention to is the readiness of each individual child for each type of learning activity. Maria Montessori called this concept sensitive periods for learning. Jean Piaget says that a child cannot adapt and organize his world until assimilations at that stage are completed enough for accommodations to occur, pushing the child toward a state of equilibrium.

The American system of public education was founded on the belief that over time children must accumulate a particular body of knowledge in order to reach a level of achievement and intelligence which will allow them to become productive members of American society. From this came the graded system used in most elementary schools across the nation, where a child is promoted to the next grade upon achieving grade-level goals and objectives set for all children. This system was set up long before the educational community had the benefit of research which shows that all children pass through the same stages of development (which are categorically different from one another) in the same predictable order, but at their own rate and often with very different learning styles.

Some children develop at an even pace and fit into a graded system better, while others seem not to be making much progress and then make what seems like quantum leaps in their learning. The latter children have a much more difficult time in a graded school setting, for their progress does not match what they *should be learning*. Then there is the child whose whole pattern of development is much slower than the rate deemed normal in a graded system. The most disturbing difficulty is when a child has not attained all of the milestones necessary to enter the next sequential grade. In a graded education system *that child has failed*.

This, of course, is the worst-case scenario, but is indicative of the underlying beliefs and problems that are faced by preschool teachers who are sending children on to public school kindergartens. Despite the fact that they have been teaching developmentally, the children in their classes may be entering a system that does not. Therefore it is necessary to alert parents who will be sending their children to a school system that may not respond developmentally to their child. Although this is becoming much less common, if this is the case, you can provide enough information for the parents to make a choice that will support continued educational success for their children, who may not have attained the required levels of achievement for school entrance.

On the bright side, many public schools are retraining their teachers in developmental practices. This is a positive trend that I hope will lead administrators to make necessary, yet basic, systemic changes—such as multi-age grouping, continuous progress curriculums, and ungrading at least up to about the third grade. At this point in development, categorical changes in the way children learn make them more like one another in reading and problem-solving abilities. It is almost impossible by the end of third grade to tell who first read at age four and who started reading at age eight. Grouping at this level will be different than grouping during the early childhood years.

It is of crucial importance that preschool teachers understand what is expected of incoming kindergartners so they will place children in a success-oriented situation. This decision cannot be reached without major input from the parents. It is truly the parents' decision, but it is the ethical and professional obligation of the preschool teacher to provide parents with all of the necessary information to help them make an educated choice.

Knowledge of the developmental characteristics of four to six-year-olds (see Chapter 2) is necessary, along with what is expected of incoming kindergartners. There are four main areas of development to be assessed:

Emotional—how a child reacts to what happens around her

Social—how a child interacts with other children and adults

Physical—how a child manipulates objects (fine motor) and how a child moves his body (gross motor)

Cognitive—how a child thinks, expresses her thoughts, and what she knows

The ideal student would be a child who is evenly developed in all of these four areas. This child would be able to successfully handle a kindergarten program without difficulty or stress. Realistically, a child who is well developed in most areas and is sufficiently developed in the remaining areas is considered a good candidate for entrance into kindergarten. Following is a list of common expectations for incoming kindergartners that will help insure success at school:

Emotional—separates easily from Mom or Dad, adjusts to change, accepts classroom routines, has appropriate level of self-discipline, does not demand undue adult attention, solves most problems without tears, can accept direction and criticism from others, is secure in her self-concept.

Social—can cooperate and share, joins in frequently in group activities without being pushed, can often solve her own problems, is cheerful in the carrying out of his "duties," can express his wants and needs, is aware of the needs of others and can sometimes place them above his own.

Physical—moves her body with control while balancing, walking, hopping, running, galloping, and skipping; buttons and zips own clothing; uses scissors; can trace and color within guidelines, prints first name.

Cognitive—recognizes some numbers and letters in random order, can count up to five objects, knows the basics of placement (front, back, first, etc.) and size, can carry out at least a two-step instruction, can listen for about fifteen minutes and stay on a subject until it is developed, has developmentally appropriate language skills: 1) receptive (understands what is heard) and 2) expressive (is able to communicate ideas verbally).

If a child is not developed enough in the cognitive area, the parent is most likely to understand that she is not ready to go on to kindergarten, for this is what we stereotypically think of as what we learn in school. It is also easier to see how a lack of physical development, especially the fine motor component, will get in the way of school success.

The social and emotional areas of readiness are less obviously connected in the minds of parents to successful functioning in the school environment. And it is here that we find the most resistance among parents of preschoolers who, in the opinion of their current teacher, are not really ready to make the transition to kindergarten.

One of the most difficult aspects of telling parents that their child is not ready to go on to the next educational level is the all-too-human response, "Are you saying that my child is less than perfect and that we didn't do a good job of raising her?" All parents feel that their children are a reflection of themselves. When a teacher says there is a problem with their child, parents assume that they have somehow failed. This, of course, is not what you are saying and, if readiness is the problem, is not even close to the truth.

Another problem is that the decision concerning a child's readiness is based on the subjective opinion of a teacher—although based on hundreds of little observations of the child under many different circumstances. The savvy parent will ask for specific examples of what you are talking about—a good question deserving an even better answer. Unfortunately, each instance you describe can also be explained in another less telling way. Only when all of the instances are put together and examined as a whole does a picture emerge of a child who might not be ready for the rigors of the traditional kindergarten curriculum.

Let's explore this dilemma through some examples. The teacher tells Mom and Dad that Harold, who has a summer birthday and is small for his age, doesn't listen well in small group lessons. But when they observe his behavior that day it is not that different from several of the other children in the group. What they can't see is that Harold always responds that way, but the others have not done so as regularly in the past. Then the teacher says that Harold often doesn't take his turn in games and activities. This could also be explained by the fact that Harold is shy or that he just didn't care to take turns on a particular day. Then the teacher says that Harold often loses control and pushes or grabs at toys. Anyone who observes an early childhood classroom for any length of time can tell you that this is not extremely unusual behavior. It is sometimes very difficult to separate normal preschool behavior from behavior that may indicate a problem adjusting to the kindergarten experience.

Taking each of these problems alone, even if they occur frequently, is not enough evidence to hold a child out of kindergarten. But putting them all together, a picture begins to emerge of a child who does not strongly display that he is ready to move on to the next educational level. What do you do now? If there is agreement by parents and teachers and all are comfortable with the idea, then the child should remain in his current early childhood setting.

Often the parent is still not sure. None of us can see into the future, so there are no guarantees that holding a child back is the right decision. But in the twenty-five years that I have counseled parents about readiness for kindergarten no one (that I know of) has regretted giving their child an extra year to develop. On the other hand, many parents who have chosen not to take my advice have come back to me later and admitted that they regret not keeping their child out of kindergarten for one more year. Often these children have been retained in kindergarten or first grade or at the very least are constantly struggling to keep up in school.

For the record, some parents have come back and reported to me that I was wrong about their child and that they are doing fine. These are the cases that I carefully study to learn where I went wrong if, in fact, I did. Children don't read the books on child development. They just unfold in their own way, sometimes in ways that we can't predict.

If there is any doubt left in the minds of parents, teachers should suggest that they speak to a kindergarten teacher at the appropriate school and ask for his or her opinion. Often parents will be invited to visit a kindergarten class in session for a first-hand look at what goes on there. They might even allow the child in question to participate and offer their opinion as to his or her readiness. Many public schools screen incoming kindergartners, which is another source of important information for parents.

An important but often overlooked aspect of the decision to hold a child back from kindergarten is to determine how the child feels. Presenting the problem and asking the child his opinion might work in a few cases, but most children at this age cannot step out of themselves enough to even conceive of what we are talking about. Despite this, they will give plenty of clues if we are willing to pay attention. You may hear telling comments like, "I don't like this class; the kids here are too big," or "I don't want to go to the _____ School."

Short Attention Span

Young children have short attention spans. This is normal and not something to be concerned about. The activities in an early childhood classroom are designed with the normal short attention span of children in mind. But sometimes a child has an attention span that is significantly shorter than that of most children. This is often disruptive to the child, the teachers, and the other children in the class.

Before any steps are taken to "correct" a short attention span it must be determined why this is occurring. Is the child in a group of children much older and merely acting her age? Does the child seem tense or nervous, causing him to be distracted? Does the child seem bored by the activities being presented or, at the other end of the spectrum, does everything seem to be going over his head? Is resisting adult direction a common pattern of behavior for this child? If the answer is yes to any of these questions, then the short attention span may be a symptom of another problem. In most cases, the attention span problem will disappear when the other problem is dealt with in the classroom.

Another crucial piece of information is whether the child can focus on an activity of her own choosing for a reasonable length of time. Many children can concentrate on something that they have initiated, but are not developmentally ready to focus for any length of time on what someone else (like a teacher) may have chosen. With time and practice, a child in this stage will learn to pay attention for increasing lengths of time. Asking for help and cooperation from the parents at home would be very helpful to this child.

Problems arise when a child cannot focus on any one task for a reasonable length of time. This is the child who flits from one task to the next without finishing and often without putting anything away. All children near the age of three will fall into this category, and it is normal for a three-year-old to behave this way. It is less normal for a child close to four and definitely inappropriate for a child near five. These are the children whose parents should be told by a teacher that their child seems to have a short attention span.

The first step is to have a conference with the child's parents. It would be helpful if this is not the first time that you have made the parent aware of the problem. If possible, try to relate simple descriptions of the problem behavior each time it occurs without using judgmental language. In this way you will have given the parents a body of information to think about before presenting the full extent of the situation.

I find that most parents begin to observe more carefully at home with your information in mind. If there truly is an attention span problem, they will be able to give you lots of examples of the same behavior at home. In fact, it is a good idea to ask parents to do so and report back to you. They will then feel that they are a part of the solution rather than part of the problem. In this way, the parent will agree that there really is a problem that needs to be dealt with and you will have circumvented the additional problem of defensive, resistant parents.

Teachers and parents working as a team will improve the situation a lot faster and more efficiently. It also makes the child involved feel more secure and cared for when he sees that all of the significant adults in his life share attitudes and concerns about him.

If after working with the child and the parents for a while, no progress is seen in lengthening the attention span, further evaluation by a specially trained professional is in order. This might be a learning consultant, a psychologist, a neurologist, a medical doctor, or a team consisting of some or all of these individuals. Using the results of their evaluation, the parents and the teacher can create a plan of action appropriate for the child.

Naptime/Bedtime

In order to fall asleep at naptime at school, a child needs to be tired and in a calm and peaceful state. Therefore a transition time to naptime is a necessity. Establishing a daily routine in a child's life is very helpful for everyone involved. It sets clear expectations about what will happen and gives the child time to mentally prepare for the next activity, including things they really would not choose to do.

The fact that a nap or rest time will occur each day and is not in question makes the transition to nap an easier task. There is no point in wasting time resisting the inevitable, even for a child. It is also comforting for a child to know that the adults in her life care enough to make sure she gets the rest she needs.

First make sure the child has had plenty of opportunity for large motor play. A period of outdoor play during the morning is very beneficial. In this way you are insuring an appropriate level of fatigue while providing much needed practice for gross motor development.

Children lose the need for a period of sleep in the afternoon at different ages. Most five-year-olds and many four-year-olds do not need a nap, but do need a time to rest. When a child begins resisting naptime, it can be a signal that his body is changing and no longer needs afternoon sleep. At that point, suggest that the child listen to soothing music or stories on tape, quietly read books, or lie down and play quietly with a few toys. If TV is something that is allowed, this may be an alternate solution, but programming must be carefully selected so as not to be too stimulating.

When announcing naptime, be pleasant and positive, denoting that this is a welcome, deserved respite from a busy day. Your attitudes model for the children and are part of their learning experience. Involve the child in preparations for the nap, such as getting out pillows and blankets, finding those special stuffed animal friends, and setting out anything else necessary to make each child feel secure and comfortable. Make sure the child understands that she will not miss anything while sleeping or resting and that you will be nearby if she needs you. You might even tell the child what you will do while she rests if you feel that this will help settle her down.

Some children like to have their backs rubbed as they fall asleep, while others prefer that you just sit nearby until they are sleeping. Quietly singing to a child or playing calming music is also very soothing.

57

Chapter 8
Social/Emotional Conflicts

Children's Fears

Fear is a feeling we have all experienced more often than we want. Most common are fear of the unknown, fear of abandonment, fear of the loss of control, fear of making a mistake, and fear of looking weak or foolish. Children worry about the same types of things that adults do, but with a specific point of view. If we remember the strong egocentricity of very young children, it will help us to better understand their normal fears and worries.

Many childhood fears are allayed when the child has a strong sense of security provided by an environment of warmth, love, consistency, and predictability. But even in the most secure situation, there will still be times when fear surfaces as a normal part of growing up.

Most children have a built-in sense of what is physically dangerous and will fear these things, such as high places, fire, and things that make loud noises. This is helpful in keeping them safe from physical harm. A small percentage of children do not have these fears, and, consequently, require more supervision and specific teaching about what is physically dangerous.

FEAR OF THE UNKNOWN

Not knowing what is going to happen next can be a very uneasy feeling. Thinking about "What if?" in a particular situation can cause fears to surface quickly. What if I can't answer the teacher's question when she calls on me? What if there are monsters in the dark? What if I can't find the bathroom when I need it?

Teachers can alleviate these kinds of fears by clearly stating how things will work in the classroom. A predictable daily schedule with clear expectations for each part of the day is extremely helpful. The children then know exactly what is expected of them, will feel more secure, and can more easily adapt to the classroom. Before the start of each activity the teacher might give an introductory statement, reminding children about what is expected (if it is an often repeated activity), or a complete description of what will occur if new behavior is required.

58

For example, to begin a daily routine the teacher might say "Who is going to remember to wait for his turn to speak in circle today? Raise your hands." Or you might try, "Remember the last time when we read a story, everyone sat on their own carpet and remembered not to distract the person next to them?"

These are positive, respectful, and gentle ways to remind children how to behave in certain classroom situations. Give children the help they need to behave correctly so that you may reward them for good behavior, rather than waiting for them to make a mistake for which you have to reprimand them.

Create a rapport with the children in your class so that they will feel comfortable coming to you and asking questions. Then if something occurs that you have not planned (and in what early childhood classroom does this not happen!), they will not have to fear what is going to happen for more than the time it takes to ask the question.

These same ideas can be applied to situations that may arise at home or in public, such as getting a haircut, riding in an elevator, meeting a clown at a birthday party, getting a shot, or having a temperature taken. As long as the child knows what to expect, he will be less fearful, especially if the information is presented in a positive and matter-of-fact manner. Don't be afraid of over-explaining because the child will let you know in no uncertain terms with "I know that!" if you have gone too far. Before explaining anything, it would be a good idea to ask him questions about the situation to determine what he already knows. This is particularly helpful in pointing out misconceptions you might have overlooked that require correction or explanation.

One universal fear of the unknown is fear of the dark. I would like to meet the person who can honestly say they have never been afraid of the dark. Young children have the added problem of having difficulty separating fantasy from reality. This, combined with fear of the unknown, makes the dark a very scary place. What we need to teach children is to allow their intellect and reason to overpower and control their emotions. If children feel they have some control over what is going to happen, they will be less likely to be afraid.

Bedtime or naptime is the most common time to deal with fear of the dark. It also occurs when a child needs to enter a darkened room. Showing the child where the light switches are or giving a flashlight to a child is often enough to make that child feel she can make the dark go away.

NIGHTMARES

At some time during their childhood, all children have bad dreams or nightmares. This is a very unpleasant experience, especially because young children have not completed the task of separating reality from fantasy. It is crucial that you explain to the child that dreams, both bad ones and good ones, are not real. They are only pretend, and you can make them go away if you want to. They will go away when you wake up or if you just think good thoughts. You can change what is in your mind. If a child feels he has some control over what is going to happen, then he is less likely to be afraid.

Sometimes a concrete reminder of their control is necessary to help alleviate fear. For example, giving a child a flashlight she can turn on whenever she feels the need makes the dark seem not so mysterious and spooky. Monster-banishing incantations can also work. Pick one that the child feels will scare away things that go bump in the night, but will not cause upset, such as "Bippety boppity boo!" or "Abracadabra monsters away!" Some adults have even given children "monster spray"—a mister filled with colored water and labeled appropriately. You may not need to go to these lengths, but you get the idea. Sometimes just establishing a routine that includes a monster check before getting into bed will provide added security.

Through all of this, remember it doesn't matter that what the child fears is not real. He thinks that it is or at least that it might be. Deal with the reality of his feelings. You can verbalize that you don't believe in monsters but, just in case, you will listen and help. The child will appreciate your honesty, concern, and respect for his feelings and beliefs. Some day you will laugh about these fears together.

FEAR OF ABANDONMENT

The fear of abandonment can often be seen in children at drop-off time at school. This is one of the factors in what is commonly called separation anxiety. One of the scary thoughts a child may have when Mom or Dad leaves is that they are not going to be coming back. The child needs assurance from the parents and from all of the school staff that the parents most assuredly will come back at the end of the day and take the child home with them.

SEPARATION ANXIETY

Leaving Mommy or Daddy (or whoever is the primary caregiver) can be a very traumatic event for a child if not handled properly, but most children left at school for the first time adjust quickly. They are secure in their feelings about themselves and their relationship with their parents. They know they will be picked up when class is over.

Going to school is rarely the first time that a child separates from his or her parents. There usually have been numerous occasions where the child was left with a relative or baby-sitter, gone into the nursery at the bowling alley or gym, or stayed at grandma and grandpa's house.

Whether or not the child has had any experience leaving Mom and Dad, she needs to be prepared for the milestone of going to school. Parents should be told to talk about what will happen, whom the child might see, how the child will get there and back, and any other pertinent information. Some helpful suggestions might be: 1) Drive by or visit the school before the first day, 2) Try to meet some of the children in the child's new class before school begins, and 3) Read books or view videos about going to school. Armed with all of this affirmational data, the child will, more than likely, feel good about the school experience.

When a child goes to school, he is taken out of familiar settings and placed in strange surroundings. This is unsettling, especially because the child's parents aren't there to fix anything that could go wrong. She may feel alone and abandoned.

When dropping a child off at school the first day, it is extremely helpful to the child for both the parent and teacher to exude confidence and a positive attitude. Children use trusted adults as barometers for the appropriateness of what is occurring in their environment. I cannot emphasize enough the importance of acting confidently, for if a child senses any hesitation on your part, she may assume that something isn't right. Even though the teacher is a new acquaintance of the child, he is in a respected position of authority that a child can easily recognize. The child will use the teacher's reactions in making her decisions.

Having friends to play with helps ease the transition from home to school.

61

If the child feels uneasy and scared, he will be soothed by everyone else acting calmly and confidently. When you act as though nothing is wrong in the face of his fussing and crying yet still lend the needed support, the child assumes that everything is as it should be. He calms down and eventually joins in the activities in the classroom.

Assure parents that it is usually better to leave as soon as possible after dropping a child off at school. Both parent and teacher can make the child feel comfortable enough to settle in, or better yet, make sure that he has connected with one of the teachers who will help him. When a parent leaves a child in the hands of the teacher, a message is sent that the teacher is a trustworthy person and that everything is all right. It also prevents the possibility of a regression of behavior because the parent lingers.

Thumb Sucking

All young children suck their thumbs on occasion. It provides comfort and a feeling of security to many children. It can, in fact, be considered a sign of burgeoning independence, for the child is providing his own security rather than depending on a parent or teacher.

Thumb sucking in and of itself is not a problem. But if it is incessant or begins suddenly when it was not a common behavior before, then the reason for the thumb sucking should be considered. There may be a new stress in the life of the child that is causing him some difficulty. In this case, dealing with the problem itself rather than the thumb sucking will probably reduce or eliminate the behavior.

Often thumb sucking has just become such an entrenched habit that the child does it even without realizing. There are no emotional overtones here, and if the child has decided that she is too big to suck her thumb and wants to stop, it can be done with support from family and school. Sometimes all that is needed is to bring the habit out in the open. A good book for this is *David Decides* by Susan M. Heitler, Ph.D.

New Baby

When a child in your class has had a new baby born into the family, there will be a period of adjustment which may include some behavior changes. It may help to share the information which follows with the parents as you support them in every possible way.

62

Each child is born into a different family. The first child is born into a family of adults who seem to be able to do everything well and know everything there is to know. The second and all subsequent children are born into a family consisting of adults and children. These children are more at ease with what they can do because they can compare themselves to their less perfect siblings instead of just their parents.

"Feeling Good"
Amanda
Age 4-1/2

When a new baby is born into a family, each person must make certain adjustments. This is very difficult for the young child, who is egocentric. He feels the unsettling loss of being the focal point of Mommy and Daddy's attention. The new baby seems to be all-important. Parents need to make it clear that they love all of their children, but not in exactly the same way. Babies need different kinds of attention than preschoolers or older children.

To ease the transition, suggest that parents include the older child in the planning and preparation for the arrival of the baby. Reading stories about new babies and lots of discussion about what it will be like to have a little brother or sister will help the child understand and accept his new role.

Divorce

It's worth repeating that young children are egocentric. When something occurs in their lives, they believe it is because of something they did or did not do. They have not developed an adult logic system, so this is not illogical to them. This causes serious emotional stress in the event of major life changes, such as divorce, remarriage, death in the family, and disabilities. A further complication is a young child's inability to verbalize her feelings. Most three and four-year-olds have not been taught the vocabulary necessary to express the complex feelings associated with divorce or other catastrophic life events.

A young child will assume he or she must have done something really bad to make Mommy and Daddy not want to live together any more. The child needs to be told over and over again by both parents, all teachers, and any other significant adults, that this is definitely not the case.

A divorce and the subsequent breakup of a household can create severe feelings of insecurity for a child. The stability of the child's whole world has been altered. She will question whether she is still loved. As the child's teacher, you can provide three critical services: 1) Reassure the child that nothing has changed at school, 2) Give the child a chance to discuss and work out his confusion and other emotions, and 3) Serve as a source of support and information for the parents.

If the opportunity arises and you feel that it would be a positive communication, you may want to share some or all of the following ideas with divorcing parents:

💜 Each parent involved in a divorce needs to make it extremely clear that their love for the child is in no way affected by Mommy and Daddy's divorce, and that the parents will always be there for the child no matter what may happen. It needs to be clear that the stability of the relationship with each parent separately remains secure.

💜 As soon as possible, it is beneficial for the parents to come up with a new daily/weekly/monthly schedule, including visitations so that the child will know where and with whom she will be at all times.

💜 It is also important that the parents take the very difficult step of working together, or at least not working at cross purposes, in all matters concerning their child. Even though they will no longer be married and living under the same roof, they will continue to be co-parents of this child for the rest of their lives. It is impossible to permanently and totally separate from an ex-spouse if a child is involved.

64

♥ Divorced or separated parents should not fight in front of the child. It increases the child's feelings of fear and guilt. It is important to remember that the child is not a source of information about what an ex-spouse is doing now, nor is the child the source of a report on what happened during a visitation. Also a child should not be put in the awkward and confusing position of becoming an emotional substitute for a former spouse. All of a parent's emotions should not be shared with a young child, because she will most likely not understand or be able to emotionally handle this responsibility.

♥ When the child is with one parent he should not be subjected to criticism of the absent parent. This hurts everyone involved. The child will resent the parent criticizing the other parent who the child loves very much. The child also may begin to believe some of what is being said—creating bad feelings, including guilt and anger. The child may now feel estranged from both parents and quite bewildered and alone.

The school or center can become a significant source of stability, comfort, and support to a child whose parents are divorcing. It is the one thing in the child's life that remains unchanged and positive. Make the school a place of security and refuge from the troubles of the world, while helping each child deal with his or her own realities as they can handle them.

Rebecca
Age 4-1/2

Remarriage

When a divorced parent of a child in your class remarries, it will require that the child once again make adjustments. This may or may not affect the child's behavior at school. As the child's teacher, you should be aware of the emotions and problems involved so you can maintain positive interactions with the child and his parents.

Remarriage of either parent is often a difficult thing for children to handle. It is helpful if they have been included in the dating period before marriage and have already formed a bond with the new step-parent. If not, this is an important next step on which to focus.

Some tips you may wish to share with parents entering into a step-family situation:

💜 It must be made clear to the child that this new person marrying Mommy or Daddy does not intend to replace the biological parent. The newcomer is a new spouse of a parent and an additional person available to love the child. This is a very difficult concept for a young child, and you cannot overdo explaining and demonstrating to the child that this is so.

💜 Another potential problem with remarriage is jealousy on the part of the child. A child may see remarriage as threatening because she is afraid she will get less attention from the parent. The child may even feel she is losing the parent's love. The security base of the child must be rebuilt, just as it was when the divorce occurred. The child must feel she can still depend on both parents and on the new step-parent as well.

🖤 A further complication in many remarriages is the blending of two families of children. It was hard enough before to get along with sisters and brothers, but now there are strangers who are considered part of the child's family, too. A lot of extra patience and understanding is needed on the part of the parent and step-parent in dealing with this issue.

🖤 Positive and loving relationships take time to develop.

66

Death in the Family

When someone close to a child dies, the child needs to be helped by the remaining adults to make sense of what has happened. The first problem is to make the young child understand the permanency of death without frightening him or her. This is most important in the death of a parent or a relative who lived in the household with the child—someone the child saw on a regular basis.

Appropriate religious references to heaven or living with the angels will be comforting if these are part of the family's beliefs or values. The school should obtain all of this information from the family in order to support them and maintain consistency in what is being told to the child. Communication between school and home is vital at this point in order to best help the child cope.

Even with caring and proper handling of the situation, it will take quite a long time before Johnny will truly believe that Grandpa is gone forever. If you watch young children play, you will see that all ills can be fixed, including death. You can "go to the hospital and get undead." Because of their belief structure, children must be convinced that what you are saying is unfortunately true.

Then the child must be helped through the grieving process, which may not come until many months after the actual death. At first, the child may seem to be handling the hospitalization, the funeral, and the loss of a loved one well. We must remember, though, that when the full realization comes, we need to be there and be ready to help the child as needed.

The adults involved must allow the child to see them sad and hurt so she will see that her own sad feelings are normal. It helps to know that you are not alone while you are working out a problem. The child is also then given the opportunity to soothe another person she loves, another important part in the grieving process.

Be realistic with the child. Don't encourage a false hope that the deceased may be returning. Don't promise that you won't die and leave her. Although this may be comforting to an adult, it only adds a new fear that the child might not have thought about. Encourage the child to ask questions. It is important that the child can still feel that you will talk to him, answer any questions, and help him understand what is happening. As much as it hurts, it is still reassuring to be able to talk about what is bothering or worrying the child.

Death of a Pet

For very young children, the loss of a pet may be their first real experience with death. They may ask many questions that seem strange to adults. They need to know the facts about death. You may need to point out that it was the pet's time to die and that he will be missed, but whenever the child wants, she can always remember him.

It is helpful for the child to take part in a burial so that he understands at least at some level that death is permanent and that his pet is not going to be coming back. It is also important that the child be allowed to talk about death and his pet as much as necessary. This is comforting, but more significantly, it aids in developing healthy concepts about the naturalness of death and the cycle of life.

If the death is a classroom pet, it is a little easier for teachers because they have all of the information concerning the pet and are more in control of the discussion. In the case of the death of a family pet, it is a good idea to consult with the parents to see how they would like the situation handled with their child. Only discuss the death of a family pet with the class if the child initiates the conversation—indicating that she is comfortable with this and that she can handle it.

Preventing Abuse

Even more now than in the past, children need to know how to keep themselves safe in all kinds of situations. Being skeptical of strangers is a good start, but a very high percentage of abuse is committed by people the child already knows. Children need more useful and specific information.

Teach the children that it's okay to say no to any adult who is behaving in a way that makes them feel funny or uncomfortable. Tell children if an adult says or does something or touches them in a way that they don't like, they should say "No, stop that," or "Don't do that," then go and tell an adult they can trust to help them. If they need help and their parents are not around, they should go to a police officer, the checkout counter in a store, into a group of people if they're alone, and into the light if they're in the dark. Scream to get attention if necessary. Warn children to never wander off in a mall, parking lot, or any public place without an adult they know and trust with them.

PART THREE

Changing Children's Behavior

Chapter 9
Basic Techniques

Teachers are often asked by parents to give advice about how to change a child's behavior that is giving them trouble at home. This is the point at which a teacher's communication skills are really put to the test. Knowing what to tell parents is not hard, it's the kind of thing done in the classroom every day; but figuring out how to say it without offending the parents or making them feel inadequate or uncomfortable is a challenge.

Obviously it is necessary to talk about the specifics of the particular behavior in question. This is covered in the subsequent portions of this section. How to communicate these ideas is discussed in Part Four of this book—Communication.

First and foremost, parents need information on general techniques for changing children's behavior. When talking to a parent who wants to change a child's behavior you might first consider some of the issues described below. These techniques work equally well when a teacher or parent is disciplining a child.

What are the best ways to change the behavior of children?

1. Change your own behavior in relation to the child.

2. Pay attention by praising and encouraging the behaviors that are desirable.

3. Ignore negative behaviors that will not harm anyone.

4. Behave in a calm and confident manner.

5. Don't be afraid to say no when no is appropriate.

6. Be decisive.

7. Work on one behavior at a time.

8. Pick your issues carefully. Make sure changing this behavior is important to you.

9. Don't give a choice to a child if you cannot live with both (or all) of the alternatives.

10. Say what you mean (literally) and mean what you say.

In order to change someone else's behavior, you must change your own behavior in relation to them. This is probably the most difficult part of changing a child's behavior. We hope the child will behave better simply because we want him to do so. Unfortunately, this doesn't work with children any better than it works with adults.

As always, we try to do the best we can for our children. This is easy to accomplish in positive situations when things are going well, but when a child has done something we do not like and do not want repeated, we find ourselves in a negative interaction. We don't want to become what feels like the bad guy who controls, reprimands, and maybe even gets angry. It is helpful to remember at this point that the most loving thing you can do for a child is what is best for the child in the long run. To say no or to limit a child's behavior will teach the child how you expect her to behave now and in the future.

Don't be afraid to say no when no is appropriate. Caring for a child is not a popularity contest. Sometimes what must be done for the good of the child is not fun and doesn't even feel good. Remember, our first priority is the well-being of the child.

If you behave in a calm and confident manner (even if you're not so sure of what you are doing), the child will assume that what you say is how it should be and respect the fact that you are in control. Knowing that the adults in the child's life are in control makes a child feel safe and secure. After all, the child believes that the important adults in his life love him and know just about everything. It is more important to provide a feeling of security and well-being than it is to be right.

It is therefore better to make a decision and act on it, even if after thoughtful consideration you feel that you may have made a mistake. A child will respect you even more if you tell her that you made a mistake, you are sorry, and this is how you plan to change the situation. A warm, loving, and assertive caregiver is usually a successful one.

You are the adult—and you are in charge. *Be decisive.* It is paramount that you believe this, for if a child feels that you are not secure in your authority, she may decide there is room for negotiation in what you have said. This encourages testing behavior and makes the changing of a behavior much more difficult.

Pick one behavior that you want to change and concentrate on that behavior first. Once progress is made, you will need to maintain the new behavior while you go on to change the next one. Explain to the child what behavior you wish to change, giving her clear expectations of what you are trying to accomplish and how she is expected to cooperate. With this kind of focus, the child will better understand the situation. Sometimes if presented in a "let's work together" kind of atmosphere, this is all that is necessary for the child to respect your wishes.

Sometimes parents complain that a child in your care refuses to go to bed at home at night. Every night when bedtime is announced there may be whining, fussing, and even screaming with lots of negotiations about how much more time the child wants to stay up, what pajamas to wear, what stories to read, how many glasses of water to drink, or anything else to draw out the process by manipulation. It would be impossible to change all of these behaviors at once, but working on one or two at a time is manageable.

Encourage parents to discuss with their child how putting him to bed is not a fun time for either of them with all the fussing and fighting involved. The child will most likely agree because children don't enjoy confrontation any more than adults do. Tell parents to ask for the child's help in working together to make bedtime better. After eating dinner suggest that parents say, "Right after dinner every night let's pick out what pajamas you want to wear and which two stories you'd like me to read. We'll put a big cup of water by your bed so everything will be ready for later when it's bedtime. This way you can play for a longer time before going to bed."

In the classroom let's say that Julie constantly moves around and disrupts during circle time and dominates the discussion. Explain to Julie that you want her to work on staying on her carpet during circle time. At first, ignore the rest of her behaviors that may seem inappropriate. Focus on giving Julie positive attention for remembering to stay on her carpet. You might even point out to the class what a good job Julie is doing even though it's hard for her to do so. This serves several purposes: 1) Julie receives positive attention, 2) her good behavior is rewarded, and 3) your comments signal to the other children that Julie is not always a problem, which avoids typecasting her as a "bad girl."

Pick your issues carefully. Make sure changing this behavior is important to you. Joanne always dresses herself, which is good, but her choice of outfits leaves a lot to be desired. A plaid skirt, print blouse, striped leggings and red socks would not have been your choice for school, or anywhere else, for that matter. Is this a battle worth fighting?

Let things go that cause no harm, even if they seem somewhat strange to you. Save your "fights" for when it really matters—lying, disrespect for self or another, taking things that belong to others, or hurting another person's body or feelings. In doing so, you will show respect for the child's individuality while still conveying your values and that you care about his or her well-being.

72

When to Ignore and When to Pay Attention

When you pay attention to a behavior, it is more likely to occur again. Behavior that pays off is repeated. From the point of view of pure logic, the solution to changing behavior becomes very simple: pay attention to the behaviors you want to encourage and ignore the behaviors you want to get rid of. Unfortunately, life is not that simple. Many of the common behaviors of young children may cause harm to themselves or others if ignored. You cannot ignore a child climbing on a shelf that may tip over, and you cannot ignore children throwing blocks at one another.

Paying attention to a behavior can take many forms. Smiling and nodding at a child who is behaving well may be enough. Asking what someone is doing, making a positive comment, or simply describing what children are doing can also be socially rewarding.

Valuable discussions can occur at the art table. Even while a child is busy creating, he appreciates the teacher's attention.

Some advice you may want to share with parents: At home, parents may want to reinforce sitting nicely at the dinner table during a meal. When a child is sitting appropriately at the table, the parent might say, "I can really enjoy my meal when you sit so nicely, Jason. Thank you," or "I like the way Jason is sitting at the table like a big boy." Chances are sitting at the table nicely will increase with only an occasional positive comment from the parent.

While supervising painting at the art table, you might make comments such as these: "Look at all the colors you're using!" "Sally, what's happening to the blue and yellow paint on your paper?" "Jesse, I like the way you're remembering to wipe the extra paint off your brush." "Robert is covering the whole paper with paint." All of these comments are positive, sincere, yet non-judgmental, and will be received as rewarding by the children.

A little splashing can be ignored when a child devotes such concentration and effort to doing the job.

It is usually rewarding to be called upon in a group situation. Just conversing with and listening to a child is a powerful form of positive attention.

73

Attention can also be negative, such as when you reprimand a child for a wrongdoing. Some children who crave attention and being in the spotlight will work for attention, even if it is negative. To them, negative attention is better than no attention. Ignoring behavior that you wish to extinguish will work particularly well with these children.

Let's look at some examples of how to *change behavior by ignoring the negative and reinforcing the positive*. It's circle time and all of the children are getting their carpets and choosing a seat in the circle. Several of them are sitting quietly in appropriate spots and are waiting patiently for you to begin. The rest are noisily milling about. The teacher ignores all the children walking about and says, "I like the way John and Shayna and George and Mary are sitting quietly on their carpets waiting for circle to begin. Good job!"

At least some of the other children will hear you, decide that they also want to be told they are doing a good job, and will quickly sit down on their carpets. The teacher can then say, "I like the way Sarah and Jeremy and Meghan are now sitting down quietly, too." Soon everyone will be sitting in the circle ready to begin without reprimanding from the teacher. It is much more effective to pay attention to those who are behaving well and ignore those who are not.

It's easier to sit still after the teacher has just said, "I like the way Johnny is sitting on his carpet so nicely."

Often in a group situation you will have a child who is calling out the answers, interrupting, and talking out of turn. Instead of asking this child to be quiet, try ignoring him, but letting him hear you say, "I'm calling on children who raise their hands to talk." Unless the child is talking out of turn simply to be disruptive, he will most likely stop interrupting and raise a hand. Make sure you call on this child to talk relatively soon and say, "Michael has his hand up. Michael, what do you have to say?" This will reinforce the behavior you want to occur.

These positive methods are always preferable, but in some situations a more direct and possibly more negative approach has to be taken. If a child is misbehaving to get attention, she will not be so easily stopped. This child is not trying to please; she means to disrupt and control the situation—and you. It is now that you must explain the logical consequence of this disruptive behavior. This could be losing a turn or leaving an activity. These negative results are enough to stop many children—most will cease misbehaving upon hearing what will happen if they don't.

There will always be a few children who still don't believe what you say until you prove yourself by actually following through with the consequence. It is a rare child who will continue when it becomes clear that no matter what they say or do you will not tolerate their misbehavior. A child who does not respond to a fair and consistent application of this technique may need additional counseling or professional support.

Giving Choices and Saying No

Don't give a choice to a child if you cannot live with both (or all) of the alternatives. Let me repeat this because it is so important:

> *Don't give a choice to a child if you cannot*
> *live with both (or all) of the alternatives.*

When you ask "Would you like to come to the art table?" you have implied that a child may answer yes or no. This is fine if "no" is acceptable to you. Adults often phrase a request to do something in the form of a question as a means of being polite. Adults hearing your statement interpret this question correctly, but most young children will interpret it literally. If what you mean is "Come to the table," then say "It's your turn to come to the table" or "Please come to the table." If there is no actual choice for the child, don't send mixed messages by saying "Would you come to the table?" This is not what you mean or intend to say.

> *Say what you mean (literally) and mean what you say.*

In dealing with children, this is actually more polite and respectful than couching your meaning by being overly tactful.

Giving children choices as much as possible encourages critical thinking, decisiveness, and feelings of self-worth, not to mention making your relationship with them a happier and more satisfying one. Children who feel they can control some things in their lives will be more likely to comply when you really need control of a behavior or situation.

When allowing children to make choices, it works best if you offer only two alternatives. "Would you like to wear the green shirt or the striped shirt?" "Would you like to have eggs or pancakes for breakfast?" You can even give a child a choice of how a required behavior is to occur, not whether or not the child will comply. For example, you have told Keith to move his carpet to another spot in the circle away from Ryan, the child he is distracting, and you are not getting compliance. You might say, "Keith, would you like to move your carpet yourself or should I?" Or a little gentler and more trusting, "Keith, I'll close my eyes. By the time I open them, please find a seat." This will also work with a group of children given the same command—"Everyone find a seat in circle," or "I want all of you to calm down and get ready to listen by the time I open my eyes."

Reserve *no* for when you really mean it or are very sure of what you are saying. *No* is always the answer when a child wants to do something that could harm himself or others.

The following philosophy on discipline hangs on the wall of my classroom as a reminder to all about how we discipline children through teaching rather than punishment.

PHILOSOPHY ON DISCIPLINE

Long-term goal :   To develop self-discipline
Short-term goals: To respect oneself
                          To respect the body and feelings of others
                          To respect the property of others

All rules of behavior in the classroom reflect these goals. Each rule has a reason that a child can understand. Our priority is not to have a quiet, orderly classroom because the teacher says so. Rather, we strive for an atmosphere of warmth, respect, order, and joy in intellectual pursuit. Most people, including children, thrive in this environment. If children are allowed, with guidance, to participate in the process of "creating" rules, "enforcement" is rarely needed.

When an inappropriate behavior does surface:

1. A request or suggestion is made that the behavior be stopped. Complete teacher control is needed only in the case of safety.

2. Questions are asked, followed by explanation, discussion, and possibly role play. Example: Why did you do that? Why shouldn't we _____? Can you think of another way to do this that wouldn't _____? What should our rule be about _____? Next time remember to _____.

3. When observing the children, catch them positively handling the same situation and verbally reward them for a job well done. Example: I like the way you're _____. I'm glad you remembered to _____. We all appreciate when you _____.

4. As a last resort, if the child is not responding to steps 1-3, she should be asked to leave the activity and go do something else. Or, in circumstances where this would disrupt or endanger the other children, this child would be asked to sit in Big Bird's Thinking Chair (a place set aside for quiet contemplation) until she calms down or can handle the situation again. A crucial element in this process is the detailed explanation given by the teacher so the child has a clear picture of what is appropriate behavior. This is not intended as a punishment; it is simply a time out to think, regroup, and rejoin. In fact, the children in my school are encouraged to sit in the chair on their own at any time during the day when they wish to think about something important.

Natalie
Age 5

Chapter 10
Power Struggles

We all like to feel powerful—and each of us seeks power in our own way. Children learn about power through play. They dress up and pretend they are superheroes who are all-powerful and can do anything they want. Little about superheroes has changed over the years, except possibly some of the names.

Some superhero play is healthy, but unfortunately, in my opinion, the attitude of some of the more popular recent superheroes seems at times to be rebellious, blurring the fact that they are supposed to stand for good against evil. I guess right now it is not considered cool to emphasize goodness. Well, at the risk of sounding old-fashioned, in my classroom goodness equals coolness. Cool equals powerful, so the path to being powerful is being a good person.

In their exploration of power, children test their limits and try on different roles to see what works for them and also feels good. Here is one place where adults can help mold children into effective, assertive, and empathetic people.

Testing and Tantrum Behavior

As a parent and as a teacher you will experience testing behavior from children of all ages. It's one thing that continues throughout their lives; the testing behavior simply changes over time. Teenagers constantly ask for things they know they can't have, like a later curfew or a new car. When they receive the expected "no!" they reply, "Just checkin'." Preschoolers do this also, but are not as conscious of their behavior, nor are they usually as verbal.

If testing behavior is handled in a firm, accepting, and patient way by the adults in a child's life, the frequency and maybe even the intensity will be lessened. When young children push at the boundaries you have set, they don't necessarily want more of whatever is limited. They may just be checking to see if you're serious about the boundary established. In this case, when handled *calmly, fairly,* and *firmly*, the child will usually settle in and accept the limits.

A second possibility is that they are experimenting to see how much power they may have over you. The decision about what to do in this case takes a little more finesse. You don't want to come down really hard and make the child feel powerless by chipping away at his self-esteem. But at the same time you will want to send clear signals to the child that *you are the adult and you are the one in charge*. This is not as harsh as it may sound. Children feel more secure when they know that adults are in control, will not allow anything bad to happen, and will be available to them if they need help. Their emotions sometimes get out of control and they can't stop crying or yelling or hitting—this is a very scary feeling.

When you help out-of-control children control themselves they are grateful, although rarely conscious of it. I have found that the children you have to discipline and control the most are often the children who are most affectionate towards you later (if you discipline correctly). I believe these children understand, even if only at a subconscious level, that you must care a lot about them if you take the time and effort to apply appropriate discipline. Children feel better knowing you won't let them get too much out of control.

Stand firm, but be reasonable. Giving away little concessions along the way will not hurt your long-term goal of maintaining benevolent control. It may also serve the purpose of easing the tension, signaling that you care.

When a child pushes really hard and uses screaming, kicking, throwing or any other extreme behavior, we call the episode a tantrum. The method used in dealing with this behavior is no different than that which has already been discussed, but a tantrum is often harder for adults to handle. A child who holds his breath and turns blue or a child who is screaming and kicking (or even vomiting—some children vomit easily when they are upset and a few can even do so at will) appears to be a child desperately in need of and deserving of our attention. It is true that this child needs us, but not in the way that seems "natural"—running over and hugging, giving attention, sympathy, and care. This is exactly the opposite of what you should do if you wish to prevent the repetition of this behavior.

A child without severe emotional problems will not intentionally do anything to hurt herself. She merely wants to make sure she has your attention and maintains some kind of control. The best way to respond to any kind of tantrum behavior is to ignore it and busy yourself with other children or other activities, once you have taken care of the immediate needs of the child and signaled her that you are available whenever you are needed.

More often than not, the child will stop whatever he is doing, turn off the tears, and join your group or return to playing as if nothing has happened. (This is the time to ask the child if he needs help cleaning up if he has vomited.) If there is an abrupt change in the behavior, as if a switch has been turned off, you can be assured that your assessment that this was tantrum behavior was probably correct.

79

If the crying (or whatever) persists, you will need to reassess. Sometimes you are just dealing with a very stubborn child and need to wait and ignore longer, occasionally offering a tissue or asking the child to join in an activity. If this is not the case, trust your feelings and respond accordingly. It is better to make a mistake and respond to possible tantrum behavior, thereby exacerbating the situation, than to ever make a child feel abandoned and uncared for. Just don't let the weeping and wailing get to you if you know that it is a performance for your benefit. If you give in to tantrum behavior and pay attention, even if it is negative attention, it will be reinforced, strengthened, and repeated.

Possession/Access

Many of the conflicts that occur in an early childhood classroom involve the possession of an object. Two children want the same toy or the same seat, or both want the first turn at using something. Variations on this problem are "he's got it and I want it," "I had it first and she took it," or "she's had three turns and I haven't had any."

Create an atmosphere of caring and sharing so that these conflicts won't come up—or at least will be greatly reduced in frequency. This is a possibility in a room full of young children who have been taught the necessary skills. (Read the section on taking turns and sharing.) "But what do I do in the meantime?" you ask.

The most powerful way to change this kind of behavior is by example. When children see you resolving their conflicts in a calm, quiet, thoughtful, and caring way, they will be more likely to attempt this behavior themselves. The first step is to intervene in the conflict as soon as possible. If possible, intervene before a conflict arises. Watch for signs of rising tension, impending disagreements, and strong emotions beginning to surface.

Through careful observation, a teacher sees that there are only three places set at the table in the dramatic play area, but there are four children playing. This is a situation ripe with the possibility of conflict over who gets to sit at the table. Be nearby and ready to help at the point when the fourth child goes to sit down at the table. Do not do anything yet. Give the children the opportunity to solve the issue themselves—they may surprise you. But jump into the situation as soon as you see there may be trouble. "It looks like there aren't enough seats for everybody. What shall we do?" you ask. If the children come up with a solution that satisfies everyone, no matter how wacky you may think it is, leave it alone. As long as no one is being hurt or slighted, the children have successfully resolved a conflict situation and should be rewarded. "Is everybody happy? Then that's a good plan."

If the children don't come up with their own solution, suggest solutions such as, "You could take turns using the chairs while one of you cooks," or "Why don't you ask the children in the art area if you could use one of their chairs?"

In the ideal classroom, you would always step in with appropriate behavior at exactly the right moment. In a real-life classroom, what do you do when it's already at the point of two children pulling at the same toy and screaming at one another? Your goal is to get the children talking to solve their problems instead of screaming or hitting.

It may be necessary for you to hold the toy until the dispute is settled. Then ask each child in turn what happened and how they felt about it. Ask how they could solve this problem so that both of them would be happy. If the children can't come up with any fair solutions, you can make suggestions. One of your solutions may well be suitable and accepted. If not, tell the children you will hold the toy until they can come to you with an idea that they can both live with. No blame is placed, no sides are taken, and the children have been given an example of how to talk through a problem. In the case of children three years old or younger, it may be more productive to take the toy away and interest each of them in something else, remarking, "You may play with this later when you can both share, get along better (or whatever phrase fits the situation)."

"Thank you teacher"
Garret
Age 4

81

A common reaction of adults to this method of conflict resolution is that it takes too much time. In my three-year-old classroom I would be doing this every ten minutes all morning long! Yes, at first this is precisely what I think should be happening. Each time the children hear the explanations and experience talking through a problem, they will be a little closer to being able to do so at a later time themselves. Even if a child is not involved in the disputes, he can learn vicariously how to handle such a situation just by listening. The time invested will be well spent and in the long run will save lots of classroom time. Your class will be developing social skills and self-discipline. You will have provided children with important lessons that will serve them well their entire lives.

In a few months, you will begin to hear the process taking place without teacher intervention. Children will still need help, for they do not know how to handle all of the nuances of all of the individuals in the class, but they are on their way to being better resolvers of conflict and promoters of a peaceful classroom. You will begin to hear yourself when one child asks another, "What's happening here?" or "How did that make you feel?" or "I'm very angry! Why did you do that?"

Chapter 11
Aggression

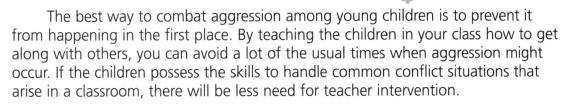

The best way to combat aggression among young children is to prevent it from happening in the first place. By teaching the children in your class how to get along with others, you can avoid a lot of the usual times when aggression might occur. If the children possess the skills to handle common conflict situations that arise in a classroom, there will be less need for teacher intervention.

From time to time, there will still be occurrences of aggressive behavior requiring teacher diffusion. There may be children newly added to your class who have not attained the level of social skills consistent with the others. Or, as the children develop, new situations may arise that have not been covered in past teachings. How you handle the situation will model for the children how they might have settled the conflict by themselves. The teaching of non-aggression begins each time a new aggression is manifested in the classroom. Old skills are reviewed and refined to meet the new challenge, or additional skills are taught as needed.

Aggressiveness in children occurs for a variety of reasons. Often with young children it is because they have not yet learned how to use their verbal skills to supplant the purely physical solutions to a problem. When one of their peers does something they do not like, they strike out before thinking. Young children are not in the habit of thinking or talking first. Instead, they use their hands or fists. Their verbal skills are newly developed and are not yet called upon as a first choice, even in positive circumstances.

We need to teach children to do the following when faced with a friend who in their opinion is not "cooperating":

1. Tell your friend to stop what they are doing and/or that you don't like it. They probably don't know that they are bothering you.

2. Tell your friend how it makes you feel when they don't give you a turn or when they take away your toy.

3. If this doesn't work, go get a teacher and tell him what happened.

4. Never hit or push another person unless it is the only way you can protect yourself. (My recommendation is that you don't offer step 4 unless you have a scenario where the aggression always occurs out of the sight of a teacher, giving the victim no recourse. Children think in black and white terms and may assume that you are saying it is all right to hit in every instance.)

It may seem strange to use the word *friend* here, but in my classroom everyone is called a friend, because either they already are a friend or will soon become one. By using the word *friend*, the implication is that a mistake was made and nothing negative was intended. It is assumed that positive feelings will follow.

By teaching children to come get you, aggression can be prevented, but the problem with this method is that in a way you are teaching the children to "tattle" and not handle the situation themselves. This, of course, is not an acceptable alternative to aggression, but it is a good intermediate step. The best result of this behavior is that it brings the teacher into the conflict where she can teach the children alternative and more appropriate ways to solve the problem. Then, hopefully, the next time the children will be able to handle the aggression by themselves.

If aggression turns to hitting, the children need to be coached in what they could have said or done that would have worked better. It is a good idea to ask children what they could have done instead of hitting. If they can't answer, then ask the children who are nearby if they have any ideas. Using this input and adding any necessary explanations, you can replay what occurred by assigning the children roles. Sometimes it is better to change the role of aggressor and victim in the role-play, especially if the child who was the aggressor is embarrassed. The purpose of the role-playing is not to punish anyone, but to teach everyone better ways to solve interaction problems with their peers.

Another reason aggression occurs is often because of anger. When people are angry they tend to lash out. This is particularly true with young children who do not have the vocabulary necessary to express their anger. Because we often come down hard on children for their aggression while they are feeling angry, they mistakenly get the idea that anger is not a good feeling. It is imperative that we explain to children that all feelings, including anger, are okay. It is how we act upon our feelings that is at issue. Say, "It's okay for you to be angry, but it is not okay for you to hit (or push, kick, etc.).

Children need to be taught how to express their emotions so that others will understand how they feel. I truly believe

"Feeling Angry"
Ashley
Age 4-1/2

that most of the time if people know how you feel about an issue they would not intentionally do things that would upset you. Initially, children must practice identifying and naming different feelings in themselves and in others. Then teachers can encourage the use of this new vocabulary in appropriate settings.

At first, one word for each emotion is sufficient, but as the children progress it is helpful to learn many more specific and subtle shades of feelings, especially anger. You don't feel the same way if you are annoyed or infuriated or exasperated. The length or complexity of a word should not scare you away if it is the perfect word to describe what the child is feeling. Imagine how helpful it would be if Ethan could tell you that he is furious because Janice is frustrating him. And think about how self-affirming it is for Ethan to be able to express himself so well and solve his own problem.

Sometimes there is a child who cannot physically control his impulses and becomes aggressive often, almost unintentionally, and indiscriminately. If you are not able to anticipate an aggressive act and step in at the appropriate moment, you must deal with the resulting aftermath. This usually involves soothing and tending to the victim's needs. However, don't forget to tend to the aggressor's emotional needs also. Despite the fact that the aggressor is the one who caused the problem, he usually does not feel good about his behavior. The aggressive child may even be crying just as hard as the victim.

I often put one arm around the victim and the other arm around the aggressor while we hash out what has happened. This makes the victim feel safe from further aggression and shows support for the child who by now has realized that she has blown it. Remember that your goal is to prevent this from happening again, not to punish the aggressor. By being patient, calm, decisive, and fair, the children learn that you value all of them, even when they make a mistake or do something terribly wrong. It also demonstrates to all of the children the faith that you have in them that they will eventually be able to do things right. This attitude promotes a feeling of group acceptance and fosters self-esteem. Once you have dealt with the aftermath, you then proceed with the same methods discussed earlier.

A third cause of aggression is a very insecure child who is aggressive in what he considers self-defense. When asked, "Why did you hit Jason?" Tommy answers, "Well, he was going to hit me (or take my toy)." You still use the same teaching of non-aggressive behavior, but in this case you must also work on building the self-esteem of this child. Tommy must feel more secure with himself and in the classroom environment before he can make much progress.

Rarely at the early childhood level do we find a bully, someone who intentionally uses her greater size or abilities to push around the other children. There may be a child who displays all of the behavioral characteristics of a bully, but does not preconceive the act and then intentionally carry it out.

When the act of aggression is taking place, we must first stop it for safety's sake. Then we can continue on with appropriate interventions. Children should never be allowed to remain in physical jeopardy. This is exactly the type of thinking we are trying to discourage. We must teach children not to use their hands or fists to solve their problems.

Chapter 12
Other Behaviors

Bad Language/Name Calling

Children use bad language for a variety of reasons. If they have heard older children, siblings, or adults using such words, they may imitate in an attempt to be grown up. They also learn very quickly that certain words trigger enormous reactions in many adults. It gives children a feeling of power to control adults in this way. Becoming the center of attention feels good and is easy to accomplish when bad language is used around adults.

It must be made clear to the child that these words are not acceptable in the classroom under any circumstance. If you feel the words are being used because of a lack of appropriate vocabulary, then teach children the correct words or at least better words to use under the circumstances.

Most children have little vocabulary for expressing anger and relational problems. In the case of one child being bothered by another, "Stop it, you're distracting me" is much more descriptive and probably more effective than other more colorful language. When a child can communicate her wants or needs successfully, she is less likely to resort to bad language.

Bathroom talk, which is extremely common in preschoolers, is a similar issue. Children learn that words describing genitals or bodily functions make many adults squirm, although they have no idea why. For the child there is no sexual connotation.

How should inappropriate language be handled when it occurs?

1. Explain that we don't use these words in school.

2. Teach the child words that are appropriate and effective in a particular situation.

3. If the words are bathroom words, but not terribly inappropriate, such as "poop" or "pee pee," but the words are being used in provocative or teasing ways, you might say, "Those are bathroom words that we only use when we are in the bathroom." This has a logic that children understand and will cut down on the use of these words without giving them "trigger" power.

Biting

Biting in the classroom is a simple issue—it is never allowed and must be stopped at once. The first time it happens you should handle it as with any other aggression, with one exception. It must be made crystal clear to the child who bit that this is totally unacceptable behavior and will not happen again. If you are running your classroom in a quiet way, with warmth and respect for the children, when you speak in a firm, urgent, and somewhat louder tone of voice, your message will come across clearly to most children. It will probably be the last time the child bites.

At pick-up time, notify the parent of the incident. Indicate that you have taken care of it at school and would appreciate it if they would reinforce what you have said at home. It is the rare parent who will not cooperate. Tell parents that you have also reported the incident to the parents of the child who was bitten. Often the parents will insist that their child apologize. This is acceptable, but the child should not be forced to say something that he does not feel, for this only reinforces insincerity.

Sometimes you will encounter a child who is a repeat biter. Have a long talk with the child about how dangerous biting is and that you cannot allow the biting to continue. If you cannot solve the problem quickly, the child may need special counseling or behavior modification. Provide the parents with the names of some local professionals who might be able to help them with this problem.

Spitting

Spitting is most easily stopped with an explanation, "We don't spit because we don't want to share the germs that are in our mouths with others." Give the children better ways to express their feelings and they won't have to resort to such ineffective methods.

Eating/Mealtimes

If left entirely to themselves, children will select, over time, a balanced diet. Unfortunately, it is impossible to always provide a complete variety of foods in school that will appeal to everyone. It then becomes necessary for adults to plan meals that provide children a well-balanced diet.

Children do not always want to eat what is served for a meal or a snack. In a school setting, there is usually not a choice of what to eat. The children should be allowed to choose whether they eat particular foods, but only after tasting them. "You can't tell if you like a food or not until you taste it," you might explain. A common reply is "But I tried it on another day and I didn't like it." The explanation is, "It is important to keep trying things over and over at different times because your tastes change. You might like something now that you didn't like when you were little (or vice versa)." Give an example from your own experience.

Trying new foods is a plus, but the children must be allowed to decide whether they like a food or not and you must accept their choice, if you want to retain your credibility, and say, "Maybe you'll like it the next time you try it. You don't have to eat it if you don't want to." Often in this atmosphere of acceptance, the child might give it another try right on the spot. Always respect the fact that some children have allergic reactions to certain foods.

Requiring children to sit at the table with everyone else is acceptable, but eating should not be connected in any way with force or negative feelings. At mealtimes where dessert is served, it is unwise to use dessert as a reward for good eating. This may create unhealthy attitudes about sweets that could last a lifetime and contribute to obesity or other serious health problems.

How then do you handle the situation when a child doesn't eat any of her meal, but still wants dessert?

Several factors must be considered:

1) Are you in control of the child's entire diet or is it a school situation where only partial control exists?

2) What will you teach the child by your decision to allow or not allow her to eat dessert?

3) What are the standards and customary behaviors at mealtimes both in the home and school environments?

Allow children to have a limited say in what they eat by helping with meal planning and shopping. Provide as much choice as possible while still maintaining appropriately balanced meals. For example, "Today for lunch we're having meatloaf. Would you like green beans or peas with that? Would you like the potatoes mashed or in chunks?" The child now feels that he has some control over what is eaten and will most likely be more cooperative at mealtime.

If a child refuses to eat any lunch and insists on just eating dessert, a decision must be made. Is it more important to maintain a non-negative atmosphere about eating, or have the child eat a balanced diet? Is this truly just an eating preference at this time or is the child manipulating in a power struggle?

One proactive solution is to not serve dessert after every meal. Dessert items can be served at another time as a snack, thereby eliminating the "eat good food before you get a dessert" dilemma.

PART FOUR

Communication

91

Chapter 13

Basics of Effective Communication

The basics of effective communication are so simple that we often do not give them their due, saying, "We already know that." Remember that the purpose of communication is to inform, to persuade, or to teach. It is not to impress, control, or force. No one likes to be told what to do or have pointed out that they are less than perfect. Making someone feel guilty or bad serves no purpose, except turning them off to what we have to say, creating resistance to our ideas. Following the basics of effective communication creates an atmosphere of trust and respect in which agreed-upon changes can be made to improve the quality of life for everyone.

1. *Say what you mean and mean what you say.*

Your credibility depends on children believing that you are telling them the truth as you see it and that each time they communicate with you they will hear the same ideas or an explanation of why you have changed your view. Be sincere.

2. *Be as clear as possible.*

If no one understands what you are saying, your communication will not have the effect you intended.

3. *Be organized and logical.*

4. *Think before you speak—a little planning goes a long way.*

5. *Think about who is listening to what you are saying before choosing your words. Choose words that children will understand.*

The very same concepts can be communicated to very different audiences (children, older adults, those with less experience, etc.) by changing slightly the vocabulary that you use. In no way should you ever speak down to anyone.

6. *Consider the feelings of those with whom you communicate.*

Presenting problems in a nonchalant, factual way with no anger or blame will foster a better relationship.

7. *Be a good listener.*

Sometimes when someone is angry or upset they simply want to be heard.

8. *Tell the truth.*

I can hear my mother now with another good piece of advice: "If you don't have something nice to say, don't say anything at all." Well, this works, except when you need to communicate something that isn't positive. Then, although you still need to tell the truth, be clear, concise, and kind.

9. *Make others feel good about themselves and they will listen to you.*

10. *Balance the bad news with something that your listener can feel good about.*

Try to end a discussion about something negative on a positive note, such as a possible solution to the problem or a word of encouragement.

Chapter 14

How to Talk So Children Will Listen

All of the basics of effective communication identified in the previous chapter apply when you are dealing with children. If children are treated with respect and understanding, they will respond in kind.

When we communicate with children, it is hard to avoid the pitfalls of repeating all of the things our parents said that didn't work on us. But without the advantage of knowing new and better techniques, we often fall back on the methods that are familiar—whether these methods are effective or not. Because most of us hear the tapes from childhood playing in our heads, a list of don'ts in dealing with children may be helpful.

Don't belittle, berate, or put down.
Don't yell.
Don't compare a child to siblings or friends who behave better.
Don't say things to make a child feel guilty.
Don't say things to make a child feel badly about herself.
Don't say, "I knew you couldn't do it."
Don't say, "You can do better than that."
Don't say, "You always do it wrong [make mistakes, etc.]."

Negativism such as the above doesn't feel very good. Being negative in your communications with children alienates them and makes them feel like resisting instead of cooperating. Be positive. Instead of saying, "Don't yell," try saying, "Use your quiet voice, please."

If you don't want a child to tip her chair, you can say this in many different ways. You can shout, "Don't tip your chair!" which isn't going to work very well. The child will stop, but will feel annoyed and aware of the lack of respect you have for her. This may only be on a subconscious level, but a clear message nonetheless. You have now pushed the child into a corner where she feels that she must defend herself.

Katie O.
Age 4

A more positive approach, using an I-message, might be, "It really makes me nervous when you tip your chair. I'm afraid that you'll fall and get hurt. Please stop." This feels better and will most likely encourage better compliance with your wishes. Children see that you care about how they feel in addition to caring about their physical safety.

Another way to handle this situation would be to say to the child, "What might happen if you tip your chair like that?" The child might answer, "I might fall over, the chair might break, etc." This helps develop the child's thinking skills (learning about consequences of actions) and indicates who really owns the problem. If the child buys into the logic, then she won't tip the chair just because you say so, but because she doesn't want to get hurt or cause any damage.

An important goal with children is to help them change their behavior to that which is more pleasant and socially acceptable. The best occasions for teaching these concepts are usually at the point where the child has made a mistake, behaved inappropriately, or has generally just blown it. You know it; the child knows it. A good way to get around this is to avoid criticizing and simply describe what has happened non-judgmentally. Talk with the child about what happened, the results, what you did, what you said, what the child did, and what the child said. During the discussion, the child may come up with an appropriate solution. If not, you have an opportunity to suggest one.

When speaking with children, use the same tone of voice you would use when speaking with an adult. Not only is this easier for children to listen to, but it is not condescending and offensive.

Chapter 15

Communicating with Parents

Always remember that the parent is the number one expert on his or her own child; you are the expert on child development and teaching. Both of these very different sets of information and expertise are necessary to unlock the mystery of each child. Neither you nor the parents are always right or always wrong. Each of you has a different point of view of the same child, and by synthesizing all the information, you are able to produce a much more meaningful picture of the child. We all learn along the way and when we work as a team this helps us to better serve the children.

Parents are highly motivated to give their children a better life, no matter what their life circumstances might be. Sometimes the teacher and the parent(s) must come together over a current crisis in the behavior or the education of their child.

When communicating with parents (or children, for that matter), it is important to determine if the person you are conversing with is ready to hear what you have to say. Will they be receptive to the learning that you are presenting now? Or would it be better to wait until later when they are?

If we looked at adult/adult communication as we do with teacher/child communication in the classroom (the mainstay of teaching), we would be very thoughtful about planning what we are going to say, how we are going to say it, and in what order we will present the facts or concepts. Sound a little like lesson planning? Maybe if we gave talking to parents the same priority that we give lesson planning, we would be more successful at parent/teacher communication.

Often as classroom teachers, we have the opportunity to report to parents an incident that occurred during the day involving their child—and our reaction to it. Watch carefully what response you get from the parent—not just what they say, but their body language and what they don't say as well. From analyzing their response, you may learn a lot about the parent/child relationship at home in addition to how this parent communicates with you.

Are they open to what you are saying or are they cutting the conversation short and changing the subject? Are they making eye contact or avoiding your direct vision? Are they using a strained tone of voice? Are they sending negative body-language signals, such as crossing arms and legs, leaning back away from you, or taking steps back as you talk? If they are doing any of the above, unless the situation is an emergency or urgent, it is better to gently end the conversation on a positive note, suggesting that you talk again soon. Try to pick a time when the parent is in a positive frame of mind and shows signs of wanting to talk.

Let's look at an example. Brewster, a five-year-old, would not let any of the children play in the building he made in the block area and was pushing them away. It was especially upsetting to the children because his building used up the entire block area. This is inappropriate behavior for a five-year-old, particularly because, as the teacher had observed, this was not an isolated event, but reflected the tenor of much of Brewster's interactions with the children in his class.

When the incident was presented to his Mom at pick-up time, her reaction was to defend her son: "Maybe he just didn't want to play with anyone today. You know, he had a rough morning before he came to school." To you this reaction seems inappropriate, but you must deal with this parent where she is in her perception of her child, not where you feel she should be. Learn as much as you can about how she feels and behaves when something similar to this occurs at home. It will help you to better understand Brewster's classroom behavior and how to better handle communicating with Mom in the future.

When is it best to communicate with parents? Ideally, in a proactive way when things are going well and before there are problems of any significance. Keep a line of communication open with each parent, often relaying progress or simply the great things the child said or did that day. Then when there is a problem, you already know how each parent reacts and interacts with you and what the best ways are to reach them. In the same manner, the parents know how you communicate and what to expect from you. They know that you give a balanced picture of their child over time and that today's conversation may be negative, but that's okay, tomorrow's will probably be positive. You can both concentrate on the problem at hand without undue concern.

Drop-off and pick-up time is an excellent opportunity to establish this rapport. An informal word at the beginning and the end of the day can work wonders.

If face-to-face conversation is not possible, telephone calls are the next best solution. Determine when is a good time to contact the parent, a time when he or she is not rushed or overwhelmed with his or her job or other children. If they can focus on you without distraction, your communication will be more effective. It is best if you can occasionally call a parent when a child is doing well, too. Enjoyable conversations promote good rapport and will make the negative or sensitive phone calls more palatable.

97

Newsletters, either monthly or weekly, are a very helpful form of communicating general information to all parents. Although this is a lot of work the first year, in subsequent years you can use the old newsletters as models and simply update the information. This is particularly easy if you use a word processing program on a computer. Generally, you repeat the same types of activities around the same times every year anyway.

Marissa
Age 4

A parent bulletin board is also a time saver for teachers. If you don't have space for a separate bulletin board, a note taped to the door works just as well. Notices that can't wait for the next newsletter can be posted immediately. Sign-up lists for party supplies, drivers for a class trip, or any other help needed from parents can be displayed so that teachers do not have to take time out of class to do these paperwork chores. Community activities can also be advertised, such as children's theater events, fun fairs, town picnics and local events, available lessons, such as gymnastics or music, and sales of interest to parents. I make it clear to all of the parents that although the notices are screened, the school does not endorse or approve any of the functions. Parents must make their own decisions.

Another form of communication with parents is a note sent home with the child. When I went to school, this always meant trouble, but that was only because notes were generally not sent home when things were going well, thereby validating the note-writing process. This can be a lot of work, but is well worth the effort if it is the only form of communication that you have with a particular parent. To ease the amount of work, you might keep formula notes on file of the types of messages you frequently use.

Formal parent/teacher conferences are a standard part of early childhood education and are useful in the late fall to present an overview of the child's current development with reference to the goals the teacher and the parents have in mind for the child for the coming school year. Spring parent/teacher conferences are beneficial as a time to review the child's progress with respect to developmental norms and to compare current behavior to the goals that were set in the fall. Even if you are in constant daily contact with parents, a conference meeting at these times is valuable. It provides an opportunity for both teacher and parents to view the child as a whole with respect to long-term development.

Dear Mrs Crawford,
I liked the time at my school. I like your haircut. I like it when I give you presents. My favorite class trip is the pumpkin one and the planterium. I like the story called, momma do you love me?, in the rainbow room. I liked all the things that you did at school and I'll always like you at school Mrs. Crawford. That's all!

LOVE
NATALIE

Create an atmosphere of open communication. You will definitely enjoy the results.

Chapter 16

Communicating with Other Professionals

We are often so busy thinking about communicating with children and their parents that we forget about the importance of good, effective communication with the professionals with whom we work. It is crucial that all staff members understand the systems, procedures, methods, priorities, and philosophy of the center so that they may work together in a meaningful way.

Develop a Center Philosophy

To work together effectively, educators first, and most importantly, must understand the philosophy of their center. It is best if this philosophy is written down for the benefit of all those who interact within the center—including staff, parents, children, and the community.

Ideally, a philosophy will be determined before the doors of a school are opened. If a school has been in operation without a written statement of philosophy, one needs to be developed.

If such a document does not exist, the administration and teaching staff of the center have an opportunity for input into a philosophy that reflects their collective beliefs and methods. We all act upon our beliefs, even if we are not consciously aware of them.

In a situation where a school is already operating with a philosophy, albeit unconsciously, it is vital that input from all of the teachers be taken into consideration. The problem of administration designing a philosophy that is not in accord with the convictions of many of the teachers should be avoided. This could lead to one of two possible problems.

The first, and possibly the more serious problem, is that some of the staff will choose not to ascribe to the center's new philosophy. (My way has worked for years, why should I change now?) This creates a center that sometimes does not adhere to its own stated policies. The philosophy that parents experience will depend upon which teacher the child is working with. This is very confusing and non-productive for the children and the parents, who become unhappy with an institution that says one thing and does another.

The second problem could be a loss of teachers who feel they can no longer work under the conditions created by the new philosophy.

The priorities at a center will be derived from its philosophy. The resulting procedures, methods, and systems logically follow. In fact, if there are any gaps in the written descriptions of the procedures and methods in the center's philosophy, they are filled in naturally and logically as the teachers carry out their day-to-day routines and activities. After a philosophy is chosen and recorded, it is a good idea for the staff to live with it for a while, fine-tuning it as they go. Then at a later time, all of the additions or modifications can be added to the original philosophy or procedural documents. This is the best way to create a philosophy that both works well and will be carried out by an existing staff.

All of these problems can be avoided if the administrators decide on a philosophy before hiring teachers. During the screening and interviewing of new employees, it can be determined if there is a sufficient match. In this way each new teacher will fit into the center envisioned by the administration.

Create a Structure That Encourages Communication

People who work together must know each other well enough in the work situation, especially in an early childhood classroom, so that they do not have to spend a lot of time communicating at the exact moment of activity or crisis.

An early childhood classroom is an active place that does not easily allow a lot of time for on-the-spot communication between educators working together. The momentum of learning (the teachable moment) will be lost if the teacher must stop, confer with a colleague, and then make some kind of decision.

Therefore, teachers who work together must be tuned in to each other on a professional level in order for things to work most effectively. This happens naturally, and amazingly well, when all of the staff share the same philosophy. They are very likely to respond in the same way to the same classroom situation, negating the need for constant communication during class. This in no way means that there will not be a need for communication outside of class time.

Teachers who work at the same school should meet on a regular basis to discuss development, issues in early childhood education, curriculum, classroom methods, and control of classroom behaviors. The larger issues of development and education would be well handled in monthly meetings of the entire staff, including administrators. This is also a good time to discuss the flow of the curriculum from a child's first entrance into the program until the day she graduates. Then teachers at each level will have clear in their minds where the children in their classes have been and where they are going when they proceed to the next level.

Weekly or biweekly meetings of all the teachers at one particular level, such as teachers of three-year-olds, would be beneficial to discuss particulars of curriculum, behavior problems that are currently being handled, and anything else involving the planning and smooth functioning of their classes. These meetings might be run by the director or a designated head teacher.

Daily meetings or simply short, informal discussions are helpful for those teachers working in the same classroom. This is an opportunity to share what worked well in the lessons, how particular children are doing, or how to handle specific situations or problems if they should arise again in the future. Sometimes this can be accomplished in stolen minutes during class, such as while the children are washing their hands, putting on their coats, or during cleanup time. If not, ten or fifteen minutes at the end of class is helpful.

Katie E.
Age 4

How to Communicate with Co-Workers

Communicating with co-workers is no different than communicating with children or parents. All of the techniques of good communication apply. Be clear and consistent in what you say and do. Refer back to the preceding chapters for a review of the basics of effective communication. These guidelines hold true for all instances of communication, including those with other teachers, although there are some specific differences for communication in the workplace.

People who work together form a family unit. They are together many hours in a classroom, often under somewhat stressful conditions. They must work in unison with regard to curriculum and discipline. Support for one another is crucial to foster good working relationships and to prevent burnout.

A kind word here and there goes a long way: "Do you need help with that?" "Great idea!" "You handled Johnny perfectly when he _____." It's easy to forget to tell people when they're doing well, and it's just as important with adults as it is with children.

There will often be a need to communicate information other than the positive. Simple information updates are necessary and cause no uncomfortable feelings. Just telling the other teachers what occurred during your activity or how Sally handled sitting next to Josh is easy. However, when what you have to say is about something your co-worker did or did not do in a particular situation, you must consider their feelings before you speak. Present the problem in a nonchalant, factual way with no anger or blame. Descriptions of what happened are often better than advice on how to handle the situation.

For example, let's say you just observed a teacher who had difficulty controlling her story group when one child became very disruptive. Saying things like, "You should have _____," or "Why didn't you _____," will only make the teacher feel defensive and uncomfortable. The lines of communication will have been effectively cut off. Instead you might encourage a discussion of the problem by saying, "I noticed Melinda was really giving you a hard time," or "The other children in the group were having a hard time sitting still and behaving while you dealt with Melinda." Simple observations such as these often invite an explanation or request for a suggestion of what to do the next time.

103

At this point, a constructive discussion could take place about the different ways a co-worker could have handled the same situation. The result is that the other teacher feels you sympathized with her plight, supported her by talking it out, and offered help when it was welcome.

Open, accepting relationships invite collegial behavior, which is the goal of any team: supporting, helping, and working together to accomplish an important task.

PART FIVE

Resources

105

BOOKS

An enormous number of books on all aspects of child development have been published over the years. I am sure that I have unintentionally left out many with positive value. Please use this list as a stepping-off point in your search for information. Look in the references and bibliographies of the books listed here for other additional suggestions.

Ames, Louise Bates, Ph.D., Clyde Gilespie, B.S., Jacqueline Haines, A.B., and Frances L. Ilg, M.D. *The Gesell Institute's Child from One to Six: Evaluating the Behavior of the Preschool Child*. New York, NY: Harper and Row, 1979.

Ames, Louise Bates, Ph.D., and Frances L. Ilg, M.D. *Your Two Year Old: Terrible or Tender*. New York, NY: Bantam Doubleday Dell, 1976.

Ames, Louise Bates, Ph.D., and Frances L. Ilg, M.D. *Your Three Year Old: Friend or Enemy*. New York, NY: Bantam Doubleday Dell, 1976.

Ames, Louise Bates, Ph.D., and Frances L. Ilg, M.D. *Your Four Year Old: Wild and Wonderful*. New York, NY: Bantam Doubleday Dell, 1976.

Ames, Louise Bates, Ph.D., and Frances L. Ilg, M.D. *Your Five Year Old: Sunny and Serene*. New York, NY: Bantam Doubleday Dell, 1976.

Brazelton, T. Berry. *Touchpoints: Your Child's Emotional and Behavioral Development*. New York, NY: Addison-Wesley, 1992.

Bredecamp, S., (Ed.). *Developmentally Appropriate Practice in Early Childhood Programs Serving Children from Birth Through Age 8*. Washington, DC: NAEYC, 1987.

Briggs, Dorothy Corkhill. *Your Child's Self-Esteem*. New York, NY: Doubleday Dell, 1970.

Dodson, Fitzhugh, Ph.D. *How to Single Parent*. New York, NY: Harper & Row, 1987.

Fraiberg, Selma H. *The Magic Years*. New York, NY: Scribner, 1981.

Grollman, Earl A. (Ed.). *Explaining Divorce to Children*. Boston, MA: Beacon Press, 1969.

Grollman, Earl A. *Explaining Death to Children*. Boston, MA: Beacon Press, 1967.

Holt, John. *Learning All the Time*. New York, NY: Addison-Wesley, 1989.

JOURNALS

For more in-depth, up-to-date information for those who would like to research a specific topic in detail—these journals will most likely be found in the library of a college that has an education department. Addresses and phone numbers for subscribing to the journals are included where possible.

Child Care Information Exchange
Exchange Press, Inc.
17916 NE 103rd Court
Redmond, WA 98052-3243
(800)221-2864

Childhood Education
Association for Childhood Education International
11501 Georgia Avenue
Suite 315
Wheaton, MD 20902
(301)942-2443   (800)423-3563   FAX (301)942-3012

Early Childhood Research Quarterly
NAEYC
1267 Child Development and Family Studies Building
Purdue University
West Lafayette, IN 47907-1267

Educational Leadership
Association for Supervision and Curriculum Development (ASCD)
1250 N Pitt Street
Alexandria, VA 22314-1453
(703)549-9110

Journal of Research in Childhood Education
Association for Childhood Education International
11501 Georgia Avenue, Suite 315
Wheaton, MD 20902
(301)942-2443   (800)423-3563   FAX (301)942-3012

Phi Delta Kappan
408 N Union, P.O. Box 789
Bloomington, IN 47402

Young Children (NAEYC Journal)
National Association for the Education of Young Children (NAEYC)
1509 16th Street, N.W.
Washington, DC 20036-1426
(202)232-8777   (800)424-2640

ORGANIZATIONS

This list contains a few of the many organizations that could provide information to you in specific areas. For a complete list of national organizations, refer to the Encyclopedia of Associations (Gale Research, Inc.) and the Regional, State, and Local Organizations (Gale Research, Inc.) edition for your area. Both can be found in the reference section of your local library.

American Academy of Pediatrics (AAP)
141 Northwest Point Blvd., P.O. Box 927
Elk Grove Village, IL 60009-0927
(708)228-5005

American Speech-Language and Hearing Association
10801 Rockville Pike
Rockville, MD 20852
(301)897-5700

Children and Adults with Attention Deficit Disorder (CHADD)
499 NW 70th Ave.
Ste. 308
Plantation, FL 33317
(305)587-3700

Council for Exceptional Children (CEC)
1920 Association Drive
Reston, VA 22091-1589
(703)620-3660

National Association for the Education of Young Children (NAEYC)
1509 16th Street NW, Washington, DC 20036-1426
(202)232-8777   (800)424-2640

National Head Start Association (NHSA)
201 N. Union Street, Ste.320, Alexandria, VA 22314
(703)739-0875

The Society for Developmental Education
10 Sharon Road, Box 577
Peterborough, NH 03458-0577
(603)924-9621   (800)462-1478   FAX (800)337-9929

CREDITS

Credo excerpt from *All I Really Need to Know I Learned in Kindergarten* by Robert L. Fulghum. Copyright © 1986, 1988 by Robert L. Fulghum. Reprinted by permission of Villard Books, a division of Random House, Inc.

Author photograph on back cover taken by Suzanne Casano Franklin.

Photographs included in the text taken by Barbara McCutcheon Crawford.

Illustrations in the text courtesy of the children in Barbara McCutcheon Crawford's preschool.

About the Author

Barbara McCutcheon Crawford is a veteran early childhood educator who has taught preschoolers for more than twenty-five years, the last sixteen years at Jugtown Mountain Nursery School, where she is owner, Director, and Head Teacher.

Barbara holds degrees in Psychology and Family Life/Home Economics, and a Masters degree in Education. She is the mother of two grown sons, Jeff and Matt, and lives in Bethlehem Township, New Jersey, with her husband Richard, two cats, a Chihuahua, a ball python, a rabbit, a guinea pig, a hermit crab, and one goldfish.

"Portrait of the Author"
Callie
Age 4-1/2

110

Notes

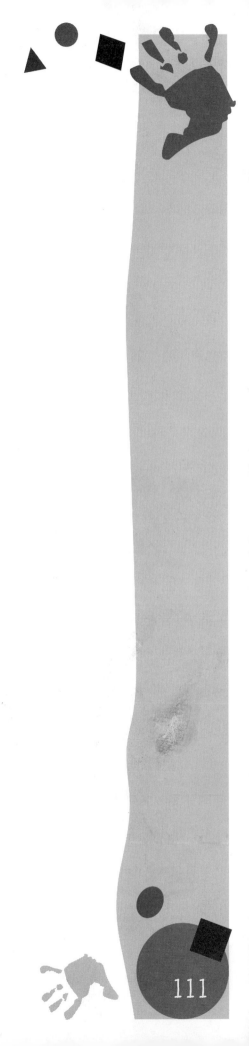

111

Notes